Leckie×Leckie
Scotland's leading educational publishers

Success guide

HIGHER
English

Iain Valentine

Text © 2011 Iain Valentine
Design and layout © 2011 Leckie & Leckie
Cover photo by Hemera Technologies © Getty Images

01/160811

ISBN 978-1-84372-802-3

Published by
Leckie & Leckie
An imprint of HarperCollins*Publishers*
Westerhill Road, Bishopbriggs, Glasgow, G64 2QT
T: 0844 576 8126 F: 0844 576 8131
leckieandleckie@harpercollins.co.uk www.leckieandleckie.co.uk

Special thanks to
Aptara Corporation (creative packaging and illustration),
Roda Morrison (copy-edit), Jill Laidlaw (proofread), Felicity Kendal (proofread)

Author thanks:
The author wishes to thank Mr JSP Gaffney for allowing him to make use of certain material originally written for the English department at Elgin Academy and Miss C McEachern and Mrs C Cunningham for their advice on textual analysis questions.

Leckie & Leckie is very grateful to the following copyright holders for
granting permission to reproduce their material in this book.

SQA for exam questions (pages 6, 10 and 18); Guardian Newspapers for the following extracts: *When Will English Come to a Full Stop* by Robert McCrum (page 8), *Reality Bites* by Elizabeth Day (pages 11, 12, 14), *Dangerous Liaisons* by Lucy Mangan (pages 16, 17), *Science Lessons Should Tackle Creationism and Intelligent Design* by Michael Reiss (pages 22-23); TransWorld Publishers for the extract from *The Greatest Show on Earth* by Richard Dawkins (pages 19-21); PanMacmillan for the extract from *The Sea* by John Banville (pages 41-3) and for extracts from *The World's Wife* by Carol Ann Duffy (pages 45, 46); Birlinn Ltd for extracts from *February – not everywhere* and *In a Snug Room* by Norman MacCaig (pages 45-6, 48); Random House for the extract from *Long Day's Journey into Night* by Eugene O'Neill (pages 51-54).

FremantleMedia Limited/Simco Limited for the photograph on page 10; Shooting Star/Eyevine for the photograph on page 16; Thinkstock Images for the photograph on page 33; Karl Weatherly for the photograph on page 41; Geraint Lewis/Alamy for the photograph on page 44; Gordon Wright/Scottishphotolibrary.net for the photograph on page 44; Colin Willoughby/ArenaPal for the photograph on page 51; Johan Persson/ArenaPal for the photograph on page 49; Jupiterimages for the photographs on pages 56 and 56; Siri Stafford for the photograph on page 56; Christopher Robins for the photograph on page 56; Nigel Norrington/ArenaPal for the photograph on page 62.

A CIP Catalogue record for this book is available from the British Library.

Shirley Scott
— x —

Contents

Who needs this book?

If you are studying Higher English this year you will already be aware of the challenges that face you. You might know someone who has sat the exam recently; you might have looked at an SQA past paper; your teacher might have talked about the 'big jump' required from Standard Grade or Intermediate English. Whatever your thoughts and feelings about Higher English, there is no doubt that it can appear a rather daunting prospect and one that a good number of candidates find difficult each year.

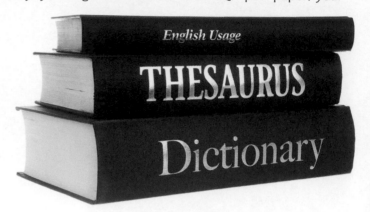

Higher English can appear daunting simply because of the importance placed on this qualification. You might require a pass in this subject in order to gain entry to the university or college course that you have always wanted to do. Potential employers will often require job applicants to have a pass in Higher English because it shows you are an effective thinker and communicator. To put it simply, our society *values* Higher English. Higher English requires hard work from you, but obtaining this qualification will give *you* more choices in life.

You should *enjoy* the experience of studying for this qualification. Whatever literature you study, and whatever language activities you undertake as part of your course, you should come out at the end with a real sense that you have experienced something worthwhile – something which has made you look at yourself, other people and the world in a different way.

This book is designed to help you cope with the challenges you will face as you work your way towards the final examination. It is designed to maximise your chances of success. Think of it as your own secret weapon in your battle against the mighty Scottish Qualifications Authority. Who needs this book? You do.

Course structure and assessment

Your Higher English course consists of two units:

Language Study

and

Literary Study

Each of these units is meant to last for 60 hours in the classroom. There is also an extra 40 hours which should be time spent on supporting and consolidating what you have learned and on preparing you for the final exam. In total your course lasts 160 hours. However, in order to give yourself the best possible chance to succeed in this subject, you *must* be prepared to spend a significant amount of your own time studying and revising.

In order to pass Higher English (the SQA calls it 'gaining a course award'), you will have to pass the **internal assessment** (the units mentioned above) and the **external assessment** (the exam and the Folio of Writing). The internal assessment is marked by your teachers and the external assessment is marked by the SQA.

Internal assessment

Language Study

To pass this unit you need to do two assessments. You need to score at least 15/30 in a test of Close Reading which shows your ability to deal with a non-fiction passage containing complex information. The questions will test your ability to understand, analyse and evaluate the passage. You also need to produce a piece of writing in a particular genre which meets the SQA's Performance Criteria. We'll look at how to succeed in both these activities later on in this book.

Literary Study

To pass this unit you need to do one assessment. You need to score at least 15/30 in a test of Textual Analysis. The questions will test your ability to understand, analyse and evaluate a piece of prose, poetry or drama you have not seen before.

External assessment

The examination

Your Higher English exam lasts for 3 hours 15 minutes. The papers are: Close Reading and Critical Essay.

The first part is the Close Reading paper (1 hour 45 minutes). In this paper you have to answer questions on two non-fiction passages. Just like the unit assessment, the questions will test your ability to understand, analyse and evaluate what is written, but you will also be asked to compare and/or contrast some aspect of both passages. This paper is worth 50 marks.

The second part is the Critical Essay paper (1 hour 30 minutes). In this paper you have to write *two* essays, so you will have to get used to producing a quality essay in 45 minutes. The two essays must deal with different genres – you can choose from drama, prose (fiction and non-fiction), poetry, film and TV drama or language. You will be writing about two of the texts you have studied during your course. Each essay is marked out of 25 so this paper is also worth 50 marks.

Folio of Writing

You have to send two pieces of writing to the SQA. One must be **creative**. The SQA guidelines specify the following possibilities for your creative piece:
*   a *personal reflective essay*
*   a *piece of prose fiction (e.g. short story, episode from a novel)*
*   a *poem or set of thematically linked poems*
*   a *dramatic script (e.g. scene, monologue, sketch).*

One must be **discursive**. There are three possibilities for this piece:
*   a *persuasive essay*
*   an *argumentative essay*
*   a *report.*

You will be given opportunities to plan, draft and redraft these pieces but they must be all your own work. You can even write one or both pieces in Scots if you want. Each folio piece is marked out of 25. It is vital that you work hard on your folio because it is the one piece of external assessment that is totally under your control.

A total of 80% of your final grade comes from your score in the exam and 20% from your folio mark. The grade boundaries are adjusted from year to year by the SQA, to allow for factors such as the relative difficulty of that year's examination. In some years you might need 50% to achieve a C, at other times it might be 47%. To achieve an A, you will usually need to score at least 67% or 68%, but again this will depend on the difficulty of the exam. You can find details of the grade boundaries for previous years on the SQA website.

Close Reading

Introduction

As we've already discussed in the course outline and assessment section at the start of this book, Close Reading in the Higher English course is assessed in two different ways. The internal assessment requires you to answer a series of questions on a non-fiction passage that you have not seen before. The external assessment (the SQA examination) requires you to answer a number of questions to show that you can understand, analyse and evaluate 'two thematically linked passages of unseen prose' (*Course Specification English (Higher)* SQA May 2010). This means that the Close Reading examination paper requires the additional skills of comparing and contrasting two different passages.

Each question in the internal assessment (likely to be referred to as a *NAB* or *unit assessment* by your teacher) and in the external examination is allocated a code letter (U, A, E or sometimes a combined code such as U/E or A/E) to remind you of the particular skill that is being tested by that question.

U questions test your **understanding** of the writer's ideas (*what* the writer is trying to say). These tend to be the more straightforward questions in the examination.

A questions test your skills of **analysis**. You will be asked to explain the techniques used by the writer (*how* the writer conveys his or her message). You will be asked to explain how the writer's use of language (which might include such things as word choice, imagery, sentence structure, sound, tone, imagery and structure) helps to get across their point of view. You will also be asked how these techniques add to the impact of the passage.

E questions ask you to **evaluate** how successful the writer is in using particular techniques or how effective they are in achieving the purpose of the writing.

Each question will have a number of marks attached to it. Unlike Standard Grade, this is a good guide as to the length of answer required from you. A '1 mark' U question is likely to require a concise response, so don't waste time writing unnecessarily long answers. A '5 mark' question asking you to compare the ideas in the two passages requires a kind of 'mini-essay'. You need to use the 1 hour and 45 minutes you have to complete this paper as efficiently as you can.

Top Tip

Always take time to read the instructions on the front of the Close Reading paper in the exam. They contain valuable reminders about what each kind of question asks you to do.

Passages used for assessment

Passages for Close Reading are always non-fiction.

This means that they could, for example, be taken from:

a newspaper article
a magazine article
a popular science book
a biography
a piece of travel writing
a report

Recent sources for passages used in the Close Reading paper in the external examination have included:
* a newspaper article on the growth of cities
* a report produced by a political think tank on Glasgow's future

- a newspaper article about why we should limit our use of natural resources
- a book which looks at our attitudes to the countryside
- newspaper articles about libraries and information technology
- a magazine article on the problem of obesity
- a newspaper article about attitudes to the 'obesity epidemic'
- a book which explores the threat to Earth from comets and asteroids
- a tabloid newspaper article.

Top Tip

Once you've started finding examples of the kinds of passages used in the exam, practise making up questions on them. Thinking 'What might I be asked about this part of the passage?' an excellent way to make yourself really focus on the language techniques used by a writer.

In order to get yourself familiar with the sort of writing found in these passages, you should, of course, look at SQA past papers and also the *Higher English Practice Papers* produced by Leckie & Leckie.

You should also research this kind of writing for yourself. Feature articles in newspapers such as the *Times*, *Herald*, *Guardian*, *Telegraph*, *Scotsman*, *Independent* and their Sunday equivalents will all include examples of the kind of writing chosen for exam passages. You can access all of these online. Pay particular attention to articles written by a newspaper's regular columnists – these are likely to contain good examples of persuasive and argumentative writing.

Understanding Questions

Types of questions: Understanding

If you have done Standard Grade or Intermediate 2 English, you will already be familiar with some of the things that you will be asked at Higher. Let's look at a selection of *Understanding* questions from recent Higher papers.

Understanding

Referring to lines 7–14, explain **two** ways in which 'That version of London would seem to be a village now' (lines 10–11). (2010)

Read lines 26–31.

Explain in detail why the writer thinks the city is 'mankind's greatest single invention' (line 31). (2010)

Explain the cause of the writer's 'depression' (line 4). (2009)

Explain why the writer believes that 'flying will simply have to become more expensive' (line 30). (2009)

Read lines 42–53. Give … any three reasons why it is difficult to define the 'traditional' British landscape. (2008)

According to lines 25–27, why does the writer believe 'a quarter of the green belt around London' should be used for housing? (2008)

Top Tip

You will always come across examples of unfamiliar or 'difficult' words in the Close Reading paper. Make a point of noting any 'new' vocabulary you encounter during your Higher course so that you then know the meaning of these words the next time you encounter them.

Notice that you are always told where to look for the answer in the passage with a reference to the line number(s). Key words in this category of question are often words like *explain; give reasons for; according to the writer, what is …; why, according to the writer …*

For all Understanding questions you must attempt to answer in your own words as far as possible. You must not simply copy down the words of the passage. Unlike at Standard Grade, you are *not* reminded of this requirement in individual questions at Higher. There *is* a general reminder to do so at the start of the question paper.

Locate, translate…

As a first step in answering this kind of question you should first of all *locate* the part of the passage which will supply you with the answer and <u>underline</u> or highlight it – remember that the exam paper is for you to use as you like – and then *translate* it into your own words. If you can't remember *locate, translate*, then think about the commands in your computer's word processing software.

find what:	
replace with:	

Let's see how that works in practice.

Look at the following extract from an article on the future of English by journalist, Robert McCrum, and the question which follows.

> Language and literature are like the tortoise and the hare. The progress of language, for example the transition from Anglo-Saxon to Middle English, is infinitely slow. The literary hare, meanwhile, leaps forward in jaunty spurts with the publication of a landmark novel or poem, say Joyce's *Ulysses*, or TS Eliot's *The Waste Land*.

According to the writer, what is the difference between the ways in which language and literature develop?   **1   U**

The first thing to do is to *locate* the parts of the passage that will supply you with the answer. Remember you will find it helpful to underline or highlight the appropriate words.

Language and literature are like the tortoise and the hare. The progress of language, for example the transition from Anglo-Saxon to Middle English, is infinitely slow. The literary hare, meanwhile, leaps forward in jaunty spurts with the publication of a landmark novel or poem, say Joyce's *Ulysses*, or TS Eliot's *The Waste Land*.

Top Tip

Remember you can mark up or highlight the exam paper in any way that you find helpful.

The next step is simply to *translate* or paraphrase the highlighted or underlined text into your own words.

Language takes a very long time to change but literature makes sudden advances.

This answer shows that the appropriate parts of the passage have been identified and that the writer's words have been successfully *glossed*.

Link question

You may have already come across how to tackle the 'link question' at Standard Grade or Intermediate. This kind of question is also coded **U** for Understanding. It is one of the few types of questions that you can approach in a fairly 'mechanical' way.

There are four steps to answering this question:
1. Quote the words which refer back to earlier in the passage.
2. Comment on how they do so.
3. Quote the words which introduce the next part of the passage/stage of the writer's argument.
4. Comment on how they do so.

Meaning and Context question

These questions usually include phrases such as 'How do lines ... help you understand the meaning of ...?'

To answer a Meaning and Context question *always state the meaning of the word or expression first* and then *quote and comment* on the words around it to show how they help you to arrive at that meaning.

Now practise using what you have learned to answer a selection of **Understanding** questions on the rest of Robert McCrum's article.

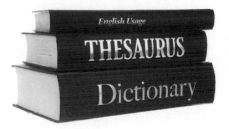

When will English come to a full stop?

Language and literature are like the tortoise and the hare. The progress of language, for example the transition from Anglo-Saxon to Middle English, is infinitely slow. The literary hare, meanwhile, leaps forward in jaunty spurts with the publication of a landmark novel or poem, say Joyce's *Ulysses*, or TS Eliot's *The Waste Land*.

5   I have been tracking the complex interaction between English language and literature through the latest online edition of the *Oxford English Dictionary (OED)*, launched last week. It's a wonderful way to pass a slow afternoon. Type in Austen and you discover that the author of *Pride and Prejudice* has fewer citations than Mark Twain or George Eliot. 'James Joyce' gives you some 2,311 citations of words from 'abraded' to 'womoonless'. There are many other surprises. Who would ever guess that Harriet
10   Martineau is the 230th 'most frequently quoted source' in the *OED*?

Leaving our literature aside for a moment, the raw data of English is also astonishing. The *OED* lists about 500,000 words. A further half million technical and scientific terms remain uncatalogued. By contrast, German scores a vocabulary of 185,000 words, and French fewer than 100,000, including such Franglais as *le snacque barre* and *le hit parade*.

15   So much for the written standard. The oral tradition yields some equally astounding statistics. About 350 million people worldwide speak English as a mother tongue. According to the British Council, the number learning English will hit 2 billion in the next 10–15 years. That's a third of mankind. Ironically, our description of this phenomenon, 'lingua franca', derives from Latin.

So is English, like Latin, doomed to the fate of Ozymandias? This is the issue taken up in Nicholas
20   Ostler's provocative new book, *The Last Lingua Franca* (Penguin). Arguing from the history of previous great lingua francas – Sanskrit, Persian and Latin – Ostler says that, over many centuries the linguistic phenomenon sometimes referred to as 'Globish', a word now acknowledged by the *OED*, must inevitably yield to historical change, and surrender its extraordinary global influence. In plain language, as a lingua franca, English is doomed.

25   Is Ostler right? Last Monday, he appeared at the British Library as part of its Evolving English series to debate this point. Inevitably, there was an air of unreality about a discussion whose outcome is several centuries away, but Ostler's claim did seem to depend heavily on historical analogies. The difficulty with predictions about English is that they are almost always proved wrong. No one, in Shakespeare's day, saw a future world role for English. Francis Bacon, the cleverest man alive, wrote in Latin, he said, to
30   ensure his place in posterity.

As well as the difficulty of gazing into the linguistic crystal ball, there's the additional complication of the contemporary IT revolution. The delivery systems of reading and writing are in such flux that no sensible person could be confident about the future state of the literary landscape. Google has just announced its state-of-the-art electronic bookstore, Google Editions. Presumably, at some future point,
35   Google readers will have privileged access to the massive Google archive. What impact might this not have on the expression of English?

The complexity of trying to predict the future of our language or its literature is underlined by an article in the latest *New Scientist*, 'Storytelling 2.0: the digital death of the author', in which Craig Mod (presumably a pseudonym) asks the question 'how do digital media change books?' Mod's answer is
40   that digital media changes 'the nature of authorship ... the very process of creation: the movement from idea to text to reader.'

According to Mod, in this brave new world 'authorship becomes a collaboration between writers and readers ... live iteration frees authors from their private writing cells'.

Personally, I doubt this, but no matter. If this is what's going to happen in the Hare-like literary arena,
45   is it not likely that we shall find an equivalent accommodation between language and self-expression in the infinitely more deliberate world of language evolution? Language is partly the product of new technology. The absolute novelty of digital media must ultimately have a linguistic consequence, though no one in their right mind would predict the outcome. In these circumstances, it might be safer to bet on the future of the tortoise.

1. Explain what the writer finds 'also astonishing' (line 11) about English. **2 U**

2. How do lines 13–14 help you to understand the meaning of 'Franglais.' (line 14)? **2 U**

3. Explain what Ostler thinks will happen to 'Globish.' (line 22). **1 U**

4. Referring to specific words and phrases, show how the sentence 'As well … revolution' (lines 31–32) performs a linking function in the writer's argument. **2 U**

5. According to the writer, what 'additional complication' is caused by the 'contemporary IT revolution.' (lines 31–32)? **1 U**

6. Explain Craig Mod's ideas of how 'authorship' (line 40) will change? **2 U**

7. What conclusion does the writer come to about language evolution in the final paragraph? **2 U**

Check your answers on page 72.

Analysis Questions

Types of questions: Analysis

Analysis questions are generally more challenging. Here's a selection from recent papers.

Analysis

Show how the sentence structure of the paragraph as a whole emphasises the idea of change. (2010)

Show how the writer's use of language in lines 9–16 suggests his doubts about the alleged 'success story of Glasgow'. (2010)

Show how the writer's use of language in this paragraph creates a tone of disapproval. (2010)

Show how any two examples of word choice in this paragraph emphasise the growth of cities. (2010)

Show how the writer uses sentence structure in lines 35–43 to strengthen her argument. (2009)

Show how the writer, in lines 35–39, creates a dismissive tone when discussing possible remedies. (2009)

Show how the word choice and sentence structure in lines 8–14 emphasise the strong feelings of those who feel the countryside is under threat. (2008)

Show how the writer's use of language in lines 4–10 creates a self-mocking tone. (2008)

Show how the writer uses imagery and word choice in lines 15–24 to convey the 'wonder of the library as a physical space'. (2007)

Show how the writer's language in lines 3–9 creates a sense of awe. (2007)

Notice that these questions frequently take the form *Show how ...*

Key words in this type of question are the technical terms *word choice*, *language*, *tone*, *structure*, *imagery*.

In order to answer **Analysis** questions, the first thing you must do is to refer to the technique(s) being used by the author (usually accompanied by quotation). Unfortunately, there are no marks for this part of your answer. The second thing you must do is comment on how the particular technique is used. The marks are awarded for your comments.

Let's see how that works in practice.

Read the following extract from an article by Elizabeth Day on reality television and the questions which follow.

Simon Cowell, the high priest of reality TV, seems to be manipulating the nation's psyche more successfully than ever before, despite the perennial scattering of media commentators who decry the genre as exploitative and socially destructive. So why are we so engrossed? After a decade of phone-in rows, vote-rigging accusations and celebrity-hungry wannabes with egos more bloated than their silicon implants, why does the British public remain so in love with reality television?

1. Show how the writer's word choice suggests the status and power of Simon Cowell in the world of reality television. **2 A**

2. Show how the writer's word choice suggests the writer's negative view of participants in reality TV shows. **2 A**

To answer Question 1, look for the words used to describe Simon Cowell and his actions, quote them and then comment on their connotations. Your answer might look something like this:

	'the high priest' suggests he is the chief person involved in reality TV, like someone who holds an important post in a religious organisation
	'manipulating the nation's psyche' suggests he deliberately controls people's behaviour, reactions and thoughts about this kind of television

To answer Question 2, look for words used to describe the participants, quote them and then comment on their connotations. Your answer might refer to one or more of the following examples of the writer's word choice:

	'celebrity-hungry' suggests they are desperate for fame
	'wannabes' suggests they have no real talent or achievements themselves
	'egos' suggests they are self-centred
	'bloated' suggests something which is unhealthily oversized
	'silicon implants' suggests they are artificial, manufactured, unreal

In Analysis questions worth 2 marks, you will usually be awarded **1** mark for each **basic** point you make. However, an answer which shows genuine *insight* and is a *sophisticated analysis* of just one feature can score up to **2** marks.

Imagery

Now you know how to answer questions about word choice, let's consider questions about imagery.

An image is just a picture in words. In the kind of non-fiction writing used in the Close Reading exam, a writer will use imagery to help illustrate a point being made or to achieve a particular effect.

To answer questions on imagery you must first of all explain the 'root' of the image and say what is being compared with what. Think about what the two things have in common and what the writer is suggesting by making this comparison. Go on to say why this makes the image effective or otherwise.

Let's consider an example. Here's the opening of the article on reality television by Elizabeth Day.

Top Tip

Make sure you are able to identify techniques such as simile, metaphor and personification so that you can respond effectively to questions on imagery.

It is a Saturday night in the northernmost fringes of London, a place where the streets are lined with Golden Nugget Chicken outlets. Outside an anonymous building with blanked-out windows, a discarded plastic bag swirls in the breeze, and in the distance the arches of Wembley Stadium soar against the darkening sky.

At first glance it seems a doleful place. But in fact, this is where dreams are made and broken. Inside that reinforced-concrete building, men in black T-shirts and microphone headsets are swarming around like worker bees, ushering a constant stream of shrieking teenage girls to their seats, testing the sound levels and the autocue, ensuring that the audience is primed to clap and scream as loudly as possible once the lights go up. Because this is where, every weekend, the *X Factor* goes live.

As the theme music is pumped through the studio speakers, it is as though the entire crowd has been electrified by a giant cattle prod. We leap out of our seats as one, arms waving maniacally in the air as each contestant takes to the stage in a blaze of strobe lighting and sequinned backing dancers. When the judges deliver their verdicts, we boo as soon as Simon Cowell says anything remotely negative and cheer wildly when Cheryl Cole gives a twinkling, encouraging smile.

You might be asked the following question about imagery:

> How does the writer's use of imagery in the second and third paragraphs help to convey what it is like inside the 'anonymous building'?

To answer this question, find the images used by the writer, explain the 'root' of these images and go on to comment on what they suggest about the scene inside the building.

A possible answer might look like this:

> The writer compares the men in black T-shirts to 'worker bees' who are 'swarming around'. Worker bees all have individual jobs to do as part of some bigger scheme or plan and this comparison effectively suggests that the men in T-shirts and microphone headsets are busy on a variety of tasks in preparation for the show.

> A cattle prod controls cattle by giving an electric shock – this effectively suggests the sudden change in the audience's behaviour when the theme music starts. It might also suggest the members of the audience are treated rather like animals!

Analysing sentences – structure and punctuation

Sometimes a question will ask you directly about sentence structure and/or punctuation, but don't forget to consider these if the question only asks about the writer's use of *language*.

In answering questions on sentence structure and punctuation, you must identify the technique that is being used and then comment on what effect it has. As always, there are no marks awarded for the reference you make – for example, you get nothing for pointing out that

> The writer uses a list in line 55.

Marks are awarded/allocated depending on the quality of your *comment* on the effect of the list. Structure your answer by referring first of all to the technique and then adding your comment.

> *The list in line 55 ('the carefree, the careworn, the innocent, the guilty, the indolent, the industrious ...') suggests the wide variety of personalities in the room.*

Any time you are asked about sentence structure, a checklist of possible features should start running in your head.

Ask yourself: Is it a long sentence? A short sentence? A list ...?

Once you've spotted the technique, think about the effect it creates. The following tables give you a reminder of different sentence features and their effects.

Feature – types of sentence	Possible effects
Statement	• conveying facts • making assertions
Question	• involves the reader • indicates writer reflecting on or considering things • a series of questions might suggest bewilderment/puzzlement
Rhetorical question	• invites the reader to think • invites the reader to share the writer's opinion
Exclamation	• expresses emotion (surprise, anger, etc.)
Command (imperative)	• instructions • can suggest friendly informality (*Bring a friend ...; Imagine you are ...*)
Minor sentence	• impact • informality • suspense
Sentence in a paragraph of its own	• impact • drama

Feature – structure	Possible effects
Long sentence	describes (among other things): • physical length • a complex process • a series of activities • something tedious or boring
Short sentence	• (dramatic) impact
List	• number of examples • reinforcement of an idea • range or variety
Repetition	• emphasis (always say **what** it emphasises)
Inversion	• changes focus/emphasis of the sentence to the displaced word(s)
Climax	• builds up to something (say **what** that is)
Anti-climax	• builds up and then descends to something contrasting with what has gone before (often used for humorous effect)
Antithesis	• contrasting ideas (look at **what** is being contrasted and why)

Language Study

Feature – punctuation	Possible effects
Capitalisation	indicates • names • titles • significance
Inverted commas "..." '...'	indicate • names • titles • direct speech • quotation • writer using word ironically
comma ,	separates • clauses • items in a list
colon :	introduces • a list • an expansion of an idea • quotation
semi-colon ;	• 'hinge' in a balanced sentence • separates phrasal items in a list
dash –	• introduces an explanation or expansion of an idea • introduces an aside or afterthought from the writer
parenthesis – – or ( ) or , ,	• indicates extra information included in the sentence (remember that you must comment on **what** the extra information **adds** to the sentence)
ellipsis ...	• indicates words missing • suggests a list could continue • interruption • hesitation

Here are two more extracts from our reality TV article. Look at them and try to explain what effects are achieved by the writer's use of sentence structure:

We are indiscriminately supportive of all the contestants. We empathise with them in a way we never normally engage with actors or celebrities precisely because they are real and because – at the touch of an interactive red button or the dialling of a phone number – we can have a say in their future. When Mary Byrne comes on stage, swathed in a black evening gown, we cheer loudly because we do not want her to go back to her checkout till at Tesco. When Rebecca Ferguson takes the floor, all sparkly eye shadow and pretty smile, we clap until our hands sting. When One Direction performs an upbeat love song in matching suit jackets, those of us who are not teenagers regress shamelessly to our adolescence. If the security guards had allowed us our cigarette lighters, we would be brandishing them now. At the back of the auditorium, several schoolgirls become breathless with excitement. 'We love you Harry,' they shout out in unison.

This is the *X Factor*, brainchild of Simon Cowell and the most popular programme on Saturday night. Each week, hundreds make the pilgrimage to the Fountain Television Studios in Wembley to be part of the live audience, and millions of us tune in at home to watch. Each week, the front pages of the tabloid newspapers will be emblazoned with headlines about Cher Lloyd's supposedly diva-ish antics or Louis Walsh's backstage meltdown.

You should have spotted the repetition of 'We … We …' to suggest the shared or communal nature of the experience.

You should have spotted the parenthesis, indicated by the paired dashes, which gives the reader additional information about how the audience interacts with the TV show (via red button or telephone).

You should have spotted the repeated structure 'When Mary Byrne … we cheer loudly … When Rebecca Ferguson … we clap …', etc., and noticed how this suggests to the reader the experience of seeing each act take their turn upon the stage and the indiscriminate enthusiasm with which they are greeted.

The repetition of 'Each week …' suggests how much the show has become a regular feature of people's TV experience.

Did you spot anything else?

Tone

Tone is sometimes a difficult thing to identify in a piece of writing. It's much easier to spot when someone is talking to you. You immediately know, for example, if the person is angry, bitter or enthusiastic. We can all usually tell when someone is being sarcastic (*'Yeah, Higher English is so easy.'*). The tone someone uses when speaking reveals their attitude to what they are saying.

It's the same in writing. The tone a writer adopts will reflect his or her attitude to their subject matter.

You need to be able to identify when a writer is being ironic or nostalgic or angry or serious or enthusiastic or humorous or …

When you are faced with a question in the Close Reading paper which asks you to 'Comment on the writer's tone …' you must first identify which tone you think the writer has adopted, and go on to explain how the language features used help to establish the tone. Look at how the writer uses techniques such as word choice, imagery and sentence structure to suggest this tone.

Top Tip

Don't say the writer is being sarcastic unless you are absolutely certain of this. Too many candidates use this as a kind of automatic response to questions about tone!

Try this

Read the extracts on the next two pages by *Guardian* journalist, Lucy Mangan. They are from an article in which she discusses the novel, *Twilight*, and the film of the same name.

Look at the highlighted pieces of text and try to explain how they contribute to the *critical* tone she adopts (it's clear she's not a fan!). The first section has been done for you.

See if you agree with the comments at the end of the book on pages 72 to 73.

Top Tip

Always look carefully at the information given to you about each passage in the exam. It can sometimes give you a clue as to the overall tone of the passage.

Dangerous liaisons

As most teenage girls in Britain will already know, *Twilight* – a tale of love between a young woman and a vampire – has now been made into a movie. It will no doubt be a huge hit. But what a shame it's not more like *Buffy*, writes Lucy Mangan.

Twilight premiered last night. If you don't know what that means, the chances are that you are neither a teenage girl nor mother or teacher of same. If you were, you would know instantly that today is the day the first book in Stephanie Meyer's internationally bestselling vampire romance saga comes to the big screen.

The idea for the book came in a dream, says Meyer, a Mormon who performed the impressive feat of typing the subsequent 500-page narrative one-handed with a baby on her lap and two other children under five playing round her feet.

Looking at the synopsis of *Twilight*, sceptics and cynics might ask if this was a dream that came to the author after she fell asleep in front of an episode of Joss Whedon's television series *Buffy the Vampire Slayer*, which also centred round the relationship between a high school girl and a 'good' vampire who couldn't have sex for fear that he would turn evil again. Sceptics and cynics who have actually read *Twilight* or seen the film, however, will simply roll their eyes at their misguided brethren and say, 'If only.'

If only Meyer had taken Buffy as her template. If only she had used that groundbreaking series as her foundation and built on it. If only there was a Whedonesque intelligence and modern, feminist sensibility informing *Twilight* and its successors. If only.

You should have spotted the repetition of 'If only …' to highlight the writer's low opinion of Meyer's work compared to Buffy … and seen that the minor sentence to end the paragraph adds impact and drives her message home. Now go on to look at the rest of the article.

What you have instead in Meyer's work is a depressingly retrograde, deeply anti-feminist, borderline misogynistic novel that drains its heroine of life and vitality as surely as if a vampire had sunk his teeth into her and leaves her a bloodless cipher while the story happens around her. Edward tells her she is 'so interesting ... fascinating', but the reader looks in vain for his evidence.

Far more important, however, is the nature of the relationship between Bella and Edward. In interviews, Meyer claims that the theme of the *Twilight* saga is choice, because Edward chooses not to behave as his nature impels him to. Alas, the only choice Bella gets to make is to sacrifice herself in ever-larger increments.

It sounds melodramatic and shrill to say that Bella and Edward's relationship is abusive, but as the story wears on it becomes increasingly hard to avoid the comparison, as she gradually isolates herself from her friends to protect his secret, and learns to subordinate her every impulse and movement to the necessity of not upsetting Edward and his instincts.

Edward, of course, has warned her not to be alone with him. To those less enamoured of Meyerworld, the implication is that Bella chooses to put herself in danger and the further implication is that she must therefore bear full responsibility for the consequences (which, in the way of vampire romances, are not entirely confined to hugs and puppies).

In the book (though, naturally, less so in the film, as she is still physically present on screen), despite being the narrator, Bella all but disappears as a character. The few signs of wit and independence she exhibits at the beginning of the book, when she is starting her new school, have long been abandoned in favour of mute devotion to Edward, which by the end is so slavish that she asks him to turn her into a vampire too, so that he needn't be frightened of killing her any more.

Now, teenage readers – or viewers, although the film loses much of the written detail of Bella and Edward's relationship, which in this case could be classed as a good thing – aren't idiots. But they are young, inexperienced and underinformed, and that makes them vulnerable to influences they are exposed to uncritically.

Edward is no hero. Bella is no Buffy. And Twilight's underlying message – that self-sacrifice makes you a worthy girlfriend, that men mustn't be excited beyond a certain point, that men with problems must be forgiven everything, that female passivity is a state to be encouraged – are no good to anyone. It should be staked through its black, black heart.

Evaluation Questions

Types of questions: Evaluation

As we have already said, Evaluation questions ask you to evaluate **how successful** the writer is in using particular techniques or **how effective** he or she has been in achieving the purpose of the writing. Recent examination papers have asked candidates to answer the following questions.

Evaluation

How effective do you find the writer's use of language in the final paragraph in emphasising her opposition to placing restrictions on people's way of life? (2009)

How effective do you find the writer's use of imagery in lines 20–24 in conveying the impact that flying has on the environment? (2009)

Which passage is more effective in engaging your interest in aspects of the environmental debate? Justify your choice by referring to the ideas and style of both passages? (2009)

Which passage do you think offers the more thought-provoking ideas about the nature of cities? Justify your choice by close reference to the ideas of both passages. (2010)

Top Tip

If you are asked about the writer's 'use of language' in a question, you need to consider *all* the possible language techniques that might have been used. Think about the features we've already looked at in this chapter such as *word choice, imagery, structure, tone.*

These questions can be evaluation questions (coded **E**), or 'hybrid' questions demanding a mixture of understanding or analysis and evaluation (coded **U/E** or **A/E**).

When you are asked how effective or how successful something is in the passage, it is usually easier to say that you do find it very successful and then comment on how the writer's techniques contribute to this. Don't forget to make your evaluation clear in your answer (*I find this very effective because* …). However, you *are* allowed to say you *don't* find something particularly effective or successful, as long as you support this view with evidence from the passage. It is perfectly acceptable, for example, to argue that you find a particular use of imagery less successful because of its rather clichéd nature.

Question on both passages

The third and fourth questions above are examples of the 'Question on both passages' that you have to answer at the end of your Close Reading examination paper. This question alone can account for 10% of the marks available in this paper, so it is very important that you are able to approach it with confidence.

This question requires you to compare and contrast both passages. Notice that you might be asked to consider just the 'ideas' of the passages, or the 'ideas' and some other feature such as 'style'. When answering a question about the 'ideas' in the passage, make sure you can identify and summarise what seem to be the main points the writer has made. Look again at the topic sentences of each paragraph – they should provide you with helpful reminders. When considering the 'style' the passage is written in, ask yourself things like: is it formal or informal, personal or impersonal, impassioned or neutral? Look at how the passage has been organised and structured; is there a point to be made about that? Does the writer make much use of figurative language?

As always, you must provide evidence from the passage to support what you say. Don't forget that it is acceptable to make reference to features and techniques you have already commented on in earlier questions.

Your marker is looking for an answer that is 'succinct', i.e. concise and to the point. You must refer to both passages in your answer, although you don't have to deal with the passages in a balanced way. Think of your answer as a bit like a mini-essay.

For full marks (usually 5) your answer should show 'a clear and intelligent understanding of both passages' and your 'evaluative comment' should be 'thoughtful and convincing'. If you show 'understanding of both passages' and include 'some evaluative comment', you should score 3 marks. If you only make 'one or two relevant but unconvincing comments' you would only gain 1 mark.

Practice exam paper

Now you have had some practice with the kinds of questions asked in Higher Close Reading, have a go at this full length Close Reading exam paper. If this were in a real exam, you would be reminded of the following on the front of the paper:

There are two passages and questions.

Read each passage carefully and then answer the questions.

You should read the passages to:

understand what the writers are saying about the theory of evolution and the teaching of it in schools;

analyse their choice of language, imagery and structures to recognise how they convey their points of view and contribute to the impact of the passage;

evaluate how effectively they have achieved their purpose.

Top Tip

For extra realism, try completing past papers or practice papers 'against the clock'. Allow yourself 1 hour and 45 minutes to complete all the questions in the following task.

Use the techniques which were explained earlier in the chapter. Once you have finished, check your answers against the suggested answers at the back of the book.

Passage 1

In this passage, which is taken from an introduction to a book about evolution, the scientist Richard Dawkins describes some of the difficulties faced by those teaching the topic in schools.

ONLY A THEORY

IMAGINE that you are a teacher of Roman history and the Latin language, anxious to impart your enthusiasm for the ancient world – for the elegiacs of Ovid and the odes of Horace, the sinewy economy of Latin grammar as exhibited in the oratory of Cicero, the strategic niceties of the Punic Wars, the generalship of Julius Caesar and the voluptuous
5   excesses of the later emperors. That's a big undertaking and it takes time, concentration, dedication. Yet you find your precious time continually preyed upon, and your class's attention distracted, by a baying pack of ignoramuses (as a Latin scholar you would know better than to say 'ignorami') who, with strong political and especially financial
10   support, scurry about tirelessly attempting to persuade your unfortunate pupils that the Romans never existed. There never was a Roman Empire. The entire world came into existence only just beyond living memory. Spanish, Italian, French, Portuguese, Catalan, Occitan, Romansh: all these languages and their constituent dialects sprang spontaneously and separately into being, and owe nothing to any predecessor such as
15   Latin. Instead of devoting your full attention to the noble vocation of classical scholar and teacher, you are forced to divert your time and energy to a rearguard defence of the proposition that the Romans existed at all: a defence against an exhibition of ignorant prejudice that would make you weep if you weren't too busy fighting it.

20   If my fantasy of the Latin teacher seems too wayward, here's a more realistic example. Imagine you are a teacher of more recent history, and your lessons on twentieth-century Europe are boycotted, heckled or otherwise disrupted by well-organized, well-financed and politically muscular groups of Holocaust-deniers. Unlike my hypothetical Rome-deniers, Holocaust-deniers really exist. They are vocal, superficially plausible, and adept at seeming learned. They are supported

25   by the president of at least one currently powerful state, and they include at least one bishop of the Roman Catholic Church. Imagine that, as a teacher of European history, you are continually faced with belligerent demands to 'teach the controversy' and to give 'equal time' to the 'alternative theory' that the Holocaust never happened but was invented by a bunch of Zionist fabricators. Fashionably

30   relativist intellectuals chime in to insist that there is no absolute truth: whether the Holocaust happened is a matter of personal belief; all points of view are equally valid and should be equally 'respected'.

     The plight of many science teachers today is not less dire. When they attempt to expound the central and guiding principle of biology; when they honestly place the

35   living world in its historical context – which means evolution; when they explore and explain the very nature of life itself, they are harried and stymied, hassled and bullied, even threatened with loss of their jobs. At the very least their time is wasted at every turn. They are likely to receive menacing letters from parents, and have to endure the sarcastic smirks and close-folded arms of brainwashed children.

40   They are supplied with state-approved textbooks that have had the word 'evolution' systematically expunged, or bowdlerized into 'change over time'. Once, we were tempted to laugh this kind of thing off as a peculiarly American phenomenon. Teachers in Britain and Europe now face the same problems…

     The Archbishop of Canterbury has no problem with evolution, nor does the Pope

45   (give or take the odd wobble over the precise palaeontological juncture when the human soul was injected), nor do educated priests and professors of theology. This is a book about the positive evidence that evolution is a fact. It is not intended as an anti-religious book. I've done that, it's another T-shirt, this is not the place to wear it again. Bishops and theologians who have attended to the evidence for evolution have

50   given up the struggle against it. Some may do so reluctantly, some … enthusiastically, but all except the woefully uninformed are forced to accept the fact of evolution. They may think God had a hand in starting the process off, and perhaps didn't stay his hand in guiding its future progress. They probably think God cranked the universe up in the first place, and solemnized its birth with a harmonious set of laws

55   and physical constants calculated to fulfil some inscrutable purpose in which we were eventually to play a role. But, grudgingly in some cases, happily in others, thoughtful and rational churchmen and women accept the evidence for evolution…

     Evolution is a fact. Beyond reasonable doubt, beyond serious doubt, beyond sane, informed, intelligent doubt, beyond doubt evolution is a fact. The evidence for

60   evolution is at least as strong as the evidence for the Holocaust, even allowing for eye witnesses to the Holocaust. It is the plain truth that we are cousins of chimpanzees, somewhat more distant cousins of monkeys, more distant cousins still of aardvarks

65 and manatees, yet more distant cousins of bananas and turnips . . . continue the list as long as desired. That didn't have to be true. It is not self-evidently, tautologically, obviously true, and there was a time when most people, even educated people, thought it wasn't. It didn't have to be true, but it is.

Questions on Passage 1

Remember when answering **U** (**Understanding**) questions you should always use your own words as much as you can.

1. Read lines 1–6.

    (*a*) Explain why the writer thinks teaching Roman history and the Latin language is a 'big undertaking.' (lines 5–6). **3 U**

    (*b*) According to the writer, what does this teaching require from the teacher? **1 U**

2. Show how the writer's use of language in lines 6–9 conveys the threat posed by the 'ignoramuses'. (line 7). **2 A**

3. Why does the writer include the list of languages in lines 12–13? **2 U**

4. Referring to specific language features, how effective do you find lines 15–18 as a conclusion to the opening paragraph? **4 A/E**

5. Explain the characteristics of the 'Holocaust-deniers' (line 22) as described by the writer. **2 U**

6. Show how the writer's language makes clear his disapproval of the situation faced by the hypothetical history teacher in lines 26–32. **4 A**

7. Referring to specific words and/or phrases, show how the sentence 'The plight … dire' (line 33) performs a linking function in the writer's argument. **2 U**

8. Read lines 33–43.

    Show how the writer's use of language in this paragraph highlights his feelings of sympathy for science teachers today. You should refer to at least two features (word choice, sentence structure, imagery …) in your answer. **4 A**

9. Read lines 44–57.

    (*a*) According to the writer, why is his book not intended to be 'anti-religious' (line 48)? **1 U**

    (*b*) How effective do you find the image 'cranked the universe up' (lines 53–54) in the context of the passage as a whole? **2 A/E**

10. How does the writer's use of sentence structure in the final paragraph emphasise his position on this subject? **2 A**

(29)

Passage 2

The following passage is adapted from an article posted by Professor Michael Reiss, director of education at The Royal Society, on the website guardian.co.uk.

Science lessons should tackle creationism and intelligent design

What should science teachers do when faced with students who are creationists? Definitions of creationism vary, but about 10% of people in the UK believe that the Earth is only some 10,000 years old, that it came into existence as described in the early parts of the Bible or the Qur'an and that the most evolution has done is to split
5   species into closely related species.

At the same time, the overwhelming majority of biologists consider evolution to be the central concept in biological sciences, providing a conceptual framework that unifies every aspect of the life sciences into a single coherent discipline. Equally, the overwhelming majority of scientists believe that the universe is of the order of about
10   13 to 14 billion years old.

Evolution and cosmology are understood by many to be a religious issue because they can be seen to contradict the accounts of origins of life and the universe described in the Jewish, Christian and Muslim Scriptures. The issue seems like an ongoing dispute that has science and religion battling to support the credibility of
15   their explanations.

I feel that creationism is best seen by science teachers not as a misconception but as a world view. The implication of this is that the most a science teacher can normally hope to achieve is to ensure that students with creationist beliefs understand the scientific position. In the short term, this scientific world view is unlikely to supplant
20   a creationist one.

So how might one teach evolution in science lessons, say to 14 to 16-year-olds? Many scientists, and some science educators, fear that consideration of creationism or intelligent design in a science classroom legitimises them.

For example, the excellent book *Science, Evolution, and Creationism* published by the
25   US National Academy of Sciences and Institute of Medicine, asserts: 'The ideas offered by intelligent design creationists are not the products of scientific reasoning. Discussing these ideas in science classes would not be appropriate given their lack of scientific support.'

I agree with the first sentence but disagree with the second. Just because something
30   lacks scientific support doesn't seem to me a sufficient reason to omit it from a science lesson. When I was taught physics at school, and taught it extremely well in my view, what I remember finding so exciting was that we could discuss almost anything providing we were prepared to defend our thinking in a way that admitted objective evidence and logical argument.

35   So when teaching evolution, there is much to be said for allowing students to raise any doubts they have (hardly a revolutionary idea in science teaching) and doing one's best to have a genuine discussion. The word 'genuine' doesn't mean that creationism or intelligent design deserve equal time.

However, in certain classes, depending on the comfort of the teacher in dealing with
40   such issues and the make-up of the student body, it can be appropriate to deal with the issue. If questions or issues about creationism and intelligent design arise during science lessons they can be used to illustrate a number of aspects of how science works.

45 Having said that, I don't believe that such teaching is easy. Some students get very heated; others remain silent even if they disagree profoundly with what is said.

I do believe in taking seriously and respectfully the concerns of students who do not accept the theory of evolution, while still introducing them to it. While it is unlikely that this will help students who have a conflict between science and their religious beliefs to resolve the conflict, good science teaching can help students to manage it –

50 and to learn more science.

Creationism can profitably be seen not as a simple misconception that careful science teaching can correct. Rather, a student who believes in creationism has a non-scientific way of seeing the world, and one very rarely changes one's world view as a result of a 50-minute lesson, however well taught.

Questions on Passage 2

> Remember when answering **U** (**Understanding**) questions you should always use your own words as much as you can.

11. Read lines 1–10.

    (*a*) Explain the question posed by the writer in line 1.   **1**   **U**

    (*b*) Show how the writer's use of contrast makes his argument clear in lines 2–10.   **3**   **A**

12. Read lines 11–15.

    Explain the connection between 'Evolution and cosmology' and religion.   **1**   **U**

13. Read lines 21–28.

    Explain the fear of 'Many scientists, and some science educators'.   **1**   **U**

14. Read lines 29–38.

    How effective do you find the writer's reference to his own experience as a learner as a piece of evidence to support his argument?   **3**   **A/E**

15. Read lines 39–42.

    According to the writer, when might it be 'appropriate to deal with the issue' in class?   **1**   **U**

16. How does the writer's use of language in lines 39–45 make his own opinions clear to the reader?   **4**   **A**

17. How effective do you find the final paragraph as a conclusion to the passage?   **2**   **E**

    (16)

Question on both passages

18. Which passage do you think offers the more thought provoking ideas about the teaching of evolution and creationism?

    Justify your choice by referring to the **ideas** and **style** of both passages.   **5**   **U/E**

    (5)

The answers are on pages 73 to 80.   **Total (50)**

Writing

Assessment

Let's start with a reminder of the two ways your writing is assessed, as part of your Higher English course. In order to pass Outcome 2 of the Language Study Unit you have to '*Compose a piece of writing in a particular genre*'. You also have to produce and submit two pieces of writing for the writing folio. The piece of writing which is assessed for the Language Study Unit can also be used as one of the two writing pieces for your folio.

Let's consider the unit assessment in more detail. The piece of writing you produce must be at least **650** words long and meet all of the Performance Criteria (we'll look at these in more detail later). Folio pieces must be between 650 and 1300 words in length.

If you have done Standard Grade or Intermediate 2 English you will already have experience of producing pieces of writing in a number of different forms and genres, so Higher English is about *refining and developing* the skills you already possess.

For your unit assessment, you can choose from the following types of writing: creative, reflective, persuasive, argumentative or report (none of which should be entirely new to you!). This means, for example, that you could write any one of the following:

- a short story set on a Dundee housing estate
- an opening chapter of novel about a girl's fraught relationship with her mother
- a sonnet about the passing of time
- a drama script involving three characters on a Glasgow bus
- a piece which explores the arguments for and against Scottish independence
- a piece which attempts to persuade the reader that schools are outdated institutions
- a piece in which you reflect on your experience of what it means to be a young adult living in Scotland today
- a report on the benefits and drawbacks of Edinburgh's new tram system.

These are just examples and there are more suggestions later in this chapter.

It doesn't matter **which** kind of writing you choose to do (although you are well advised to attempt something at which you are already reasonably competent), what *is* important is that the writing is **your** work. Your teacher should ask you for the following at each stage of the writing process, in order to guarantee the authenticity of what you produce: a draft title, proposals, an outline plan, a first draft, a final version.

A draft title, proposals and outline plan for a persuasive piece of writing might look something like this:

Date:	Pupil Name:	Language Study Unit – Writing
Proposed Title: *Education 2.0 – Why our schools are failing to pass the test*		Genre: Persuasive
Proposals In this essay I am going to persuade the reader to agree with my point of view that schools are no longer fit for purpose and do not provide their pupils with an education experience which is relevant to the needs of society in the twenty first century. I will show that they are institutions which have remained largely unchanged since the early years of the last century, and that our insistence on gathering large groups of young people together in huge buildings and then dividing them into groups based on arbitrary principles, rules and flawed statistics is no longer an effective way of educating young people today. I will also look at how information technology is radically altering how we learn and how we interact with others, and that this means we need a complete overhaul of what we want our schools to do. Teacher's initials: Date:		

Date:	Name:	Language Study – Writing
Draft Title: *Education 2.0 Why our schools are failing to pass the test*		Genre: Persuasive

Outline

Introduction:

- Description of typical school day from thirty years ago (classes, timetables, buildings, bells, etc.) – shows how little pupils' experience has changed – contrast with radical changes in society and technology – suggest schools need to change.

Points I intend to make:

- Maintaining school buildings is a huge drain on the public purse (use local authority statistics).
- Very few of us will ever work in such a large 'communities' again – why corral young people into these buildings? Once we leave school most people now work in small teams and more than ever are working from home.
- Acknowledge the counter argument about the 'socialising' effect of schools, but dismiss this with reference to the negative aspects of school life such as bullying.
- Examples of successful learning outwith school.
- Point out how Information Technology is embedded within our lives – ref. to internet, social networking – how this has changed the way we interact with others.
- Point out how Information Technology has changed the way we learn – Wikipedia, etc. – schools own greater use of websites, Virtual Learning Environments, GLOW – so why the need for 'traditional' classrooms?
- Health risks – easy for viruses such as flu to spread in large schools, etc.

Conclusion

- Reiterate points made and end with strong closing statement.

Teacher's initials:

Date:

Once your teacher has had a look at your proposals you can start work on a first draft. Remember that a word-processed draft will be easier for you to edit and amend before you produce the final version.

Let's see what the introductory paragraphs of our 'Persuasive' piece might look like. Remember to make use of the language techniques you have come across in your study of Close Reading passages.

Education 2.0 Why our schools are failing to pass the test

First draft

[Starts with a command – involves the reader] Picture the scene. The dutiful pupil dressed in full school uniform arrives at her local secondary school. It is a large concrete and glass box; a box she shares with 1000 other dutiful souls. Her day is mapped out before her; a day delineated by the grid squares of her timetable. A bell rings and she dutifully makes her way to her registration room. Another bell rings and she dutifully carries her bag full of jotters and folders to her first class. Her teacher hands out the textbooks and the pupil dutifully begins to work through the examples …

[Suggests 'restriction']

[Word choice suggests unflattering image of school building]

[Connotations of lack of freedom]

[Repetition of 'dutiful'/ 'dutifully' suggests someone meekly following instructions] This dutiful pupil is receiving her education in a Scottish secondary school in 2011, but the year could have been 2001, 1991, 1981 or 1971. Outwith school, however, things are very different for this pupil compared with her sisters of forty, thirty, twenty or even ten years ago. In school, she is hemmed in; at home she can roam the digital world at will. This same dutiful pupil goes home to watch her favourite TV shows online, updates her facebook profile and chats to friends and relatives in Germany and Australia. She then sharpens up her guitar playing with a quick tutorial from a useful website and ends her day by making another entry on her blog. How can imprisoning her in a concrete and glass box for six years possibly be to the benefit of this young person?

[List of dates suggests unchanging nature of school experience over time]

[Balanced sentence around a semi-colon 'hinge'.]

[Emotive language to elicit sympathy from the reader]

[Paragraph ends with a thought-provoking question]

Once a first draft has been completed, you should ensure it contains the features required for an effective piece of writing at this level. Here is a checklist for Persuasive writing:

Discursive Persuasive	✓
strong opening statement	
clear structure	
effective use of linkage between sections/arguments	
emotive vocabulary	
arguments supported by evidence (statistics, etc.) where appropriate	
acknowledgement and rejection of any counter-arguments	
direct address to the reader	
repetition	
climax	
contrast	
contrast within a list	
use of analogy and/or illustration	
listing for effect (especially in groups of three)	
effective use of imagery	
gives a clear sense that the writer is *convinced* of his/her case	

Discursive Persuasive	✓
effective use of 'attitude markers': *Surely, ... Clearly, ... Happily, ...*	
strong closing statement	
sources consulted are clearly stated	

Once you have completed a first draft of your writing, your teacher will be able to give you feedback. This feedback will usually suggest improvements that you might make to your piece. You might be asked to look again at the way you have structured your writing (perhaps you need to reorder your ideas) or you might be told that your punctuation and spelling are not yet 'consistently accurate'. Your teacher is **not**, however, allowed to indicate specific, individual errors for you to go away and correct. Proof-reading and editing of your work are *your* responsibility.

Once you have handed in your final version it will be assessed against the Performance Criteria. The Performance Criteria as set down in the SQA Higher English Arrangements document are as follows:

Performance Criteria	Achieved?
Content Content is relevant and appropriate for purpose and audience, reveals depth and complexity of thought and sustained development.	
Structure Structure is effective and appropriate for purpose, audience and genre; content is sequenced and organised in ways which assist impact.	
Expression Capable use of techniques relevant to the genre and effective choice of words and sentence structures sustain a style and tone which clearly communicates a point of view/stance consistent with purpose and audience.	
Technical accuracy Spelling, grammar and punctuation are consistently accurate.	

Your writing must achieve all four of the criteria to pass. Some key concepts in the Performance Criteria are:

'depth and complexity of thought' – this is a clear indicator that you have to produce a piece of writing which contains ideas which are **more sophisticated** than you probably needed to include in your writing at Standard Grade or at Intermediate 2 level.

'Content is ... organised in ways which assist impact' – a reminder that you should **construct** your piece for maximum effect. You must *plan* your piece effectively.

'effective choice of words and sentence structures' – select your **vocabulary** carefully (but don't overuse the thesaurus!) and use the sentence structure techniques you are already familiar with from Close Reading and Textual Analysis.

'consistently accurate' – this means your spelling, punctuation, etc., have to be more accurate than is allowed in the Critical Essay in the exam (where they only have to be '*sufficiently* accurate'). So get into the habit of taking time to check your spelling, grammar and punctuation carefully at each stage of the writing process. Remember this is **your** responsibility.

In order to achieve a pass, the piece **must** be at least **650** words long (this does not apply to poetry).

Features of each genre

Once you have decided what kind of writing you want to do, here's a reminder of the features and techniques to use. We've already looked at those required for persuasive writing, so here we consider a short story, a reflective piece, an argumentative piece and a drama script. An opening with comments and a checklist for each genre are provided for you, and you could try continuing each piece for practice. Remember to make use of the appropriate techniques.

The Hunted
(Short story)

First draft

> Story starts 'in medias res' – in the middle of the action

She turned the key. Nothing. She turned the key again. Still nothing. A small bubble of fear tried to rise in her chest. She willed herself to ignore it and turned the key again. This time the engine coughed and caught. She felt the small bubble burst and she pressed her foot down on the accelerator.

> Minor sentence helps create a tense atmosphere

> Personification suggesting hostility

She hated driving on her own through this part of the city. She hated the empty streets; the feeling that people had given up on it. Ugly houses leered at her from either side. *Everything's fine. This is something you can do. It's not going to happen again.*

> *Showing* the reader she's engaged or married, rather than *telling* them

She glanced nervously in the mirror and adjusted it a fraction. The diamond on her left hand briefly caught the light as she changed gear. *Normal, normal, normal. Ordinary. It's a day like any other. It's a journey like any other. You've done this a hundred times before. Think about next week. Think about Alan. Think!*

> Italics to indicate the character's thoughts

She looked in the mirror again.

A black car.

Something quivered inside her. *It was a coincidence – that was all. There must be a hundred black cars in the city, a thousand.* She gripped the wheel more tightly.

She looked in the mirror again.

Creative Short Story	✓
limited setting	
definite shape or structure	
few characters	
action takes place over a relatively short space of time	
limited number of plot 'events'	
use of imagery – *metaphor, simile, personification …*	
use of symbolism	
provides insight into a character's life/thoughts/feelings	
reveals or *shows* the reader things rather than telling them	

Top Tip

In this kind of writing, make use of the techniques you have learned about as part of your study of prose fiction and the textual analysis of prose.

Creative Short Story	✔
use of believable dialogue to bring characters to life	
credible ending	
some sort of change evident (from the fortunes/situation/ mind-set of the character(s) at the story's start)	
spelling is consistently accurate	
punctuation is consistently accurate	
sentence construction is consistently accurate	

Relative Values (Reflective)

First draft

Stimulus for the reflection → It's not much to look at: just a small lapel badge made up of the letters N.U.M.

Repeated structure emphasises what was important in his life → *National Union of Mineworkers*; and yet every time I pick it up I am reminded of the man who wore it. A man with thirty years service 'man and boy' to his local pit. A man who loved the camaraderie of it all. A man who loved his pipe band and his football team. A man who loved his family – but never told them. Loyal to his union, to his mates, to his wife and children. Loyalty as much a part of him as the dust in his lungs that did for him in the end.

Appropriate use of imagery linked to mining → I peer down the dim shaft of time and try to see the man that he was but I can't. I sit at my laptop looking at his picture and I feel the accumulated years lying in layer upon layer between his youth and mine. And I think about the differences between us ...

The writer introduces the idea which will be at the heart of this essay

Creative Reflective	✔
captures the reader's interest	
deals with a single idea/insight/experience	
evidence of reflection on knowledge/thoughts/feelings caused by the subject of the essay	
uses a personal tone	
the reader gets a clear sense of the writer's personality	
gives a sense of the writer really *thinking* about the subject of the essay	
states what has been realised/learned by the writer	
shows difference between how experience/event was viewed *then* and how it is viewed *now* (if appropriate)	
uses word choice to create particular effects	
uses imagery to create particular effects	
uses sentence structure to create particular effects	
spelling is consistently accurate	
sentence construction is consistently accurate	

Top Tip

Start writing your own blog. Use it as a way of sharing your reflections on your experiences.

Tempestuous Times – are wind farms a blot on the Scottish landscape?
(Argumentative)

First draft

Introductory paragraph sets out the context for the essay

As we move further into the twenty-first century, it is clear that we must decide how our energy needs will be met in the coming years. At the moment we think nothing of switching on a light, a cooker, a computer – but how can we ensure that our insatiable demand for power can be satisfied in the future? Fossil fuels will disappear in 50 years according to some experts. That means no more power stations fuelled by coal or gas so it is vital that we find alternative means of generating electricity if that light, cooker and computer are still going to be available to us half a century from now.

Renewable forms of energy sources such as wind, wave and hydro will all play a significant role in providing us with energy in future. Will this mean more and more 'wind farms' being constructed in Scotland's countryside? Proponents of such schemes trumpet their 'eco-friendly' qualities whilst others warn against the damage that might be done to precious landscape.

The two arguments that will be considered in the essay

Which side is correct?

Use of official statistics

The Scottish Government want '80% of Scotland's gross annual electricity consumption' to come from renewable resources by 2020. Supporters of wind farms say that this means that we must build more wind turbines.

Discursive Argumentative	✓
introduces the topic clearly	
makes use of *at least* two arguments related to the topic	
has a clear, logical structure	
makes effective use of linkage between sections/arguments	
arguments supported by evidence (statistics, etc.) where appropriate	
effective use of transition markers (*however, furthermore, in addition to this, despite this* …)	
uses an appropriate tone (conveyed through appropriate word choice and other language features)	
uses comparisons	
arguments disproved by evidence (statistics, etc.) where appropriate	
arrives at a clear conclusion having evaluated the evidence	
spelling is consistently accurate	
punctuation is consistently accurate	
sentence construction is consistently accurate	
sources consulted are clearly stated	

Top Tip

In this kind of writing, remember to make use of the techniques you've learned about in your Close Reading work.

Flatmates
Drama script

First draft

Characters:

Claire – a well-dressed, tall, dark-haired young woman in her mid-twenties. She has the air of someone always in control. Her speech should sound 'educated' and precise.

Rebecca – the same age as Claire but shorter. Her demeanour suggests a very relaxed attitude to life in general.

Amy – prospective flatmate of Claire and Rebecca

It is a weekday morning in the living room of a flat in Glasgow. The room is clean and tidy. There is a sofa facing a wall on which there is a flat screen television above a fireplace. There are two 'modern' armchairs beside a coffee table. On the coffee table there is an open laptop and a (very) neatly stacked pile of magazines. The general impression is of orderliness. The only object which seems out of place is the empty beer can lying on its side on the floor beside the sofa.

Claire enters. She glances around the room, walks over to the coffee table and straightens the pile of magazines that do not need straightening. Once she is satisfied, she looks around the room once more, biting her lower lip.

Claire: (*noticing the beer can on the floor*) Oh not again! (*Shouting*) Becca! Get through here and look at this!

Rebecca: (*Off*) What?

Claire: (*picks up the can and holds it distastefully at arm's length*) This! What sort of impression do you think this is going to make?

Rebecca enters. She is wearing a dressing gown. Her hair is unkempt and there is clear evidence of last night's make-up all over her face. She walks wearily past Claire. She studiously ignores Claire's outstretched arm, which still holds the beer can, and slumps into an armchair.

Claire: Well?

Rebecca: (*eyes closed*) Aw jeez, Claire. Get a life. What is it this time? Your IKEA catalogues no arranged in date order on the table? The curtains two centimetres too far apart?

Claire: Don't be like that! You know exactly what I am talking about.

Rebecca: (*opening one eye and seemingly acknowledging the beer can for the first time*) Oh, is that all? Ah thought it was something serious.

Language Study

Claire:	This is serious. You know she's coming round at ten thirty sharp. That means any minute now. Do I need to remind you how much we need a third to split the rent? Have you forgotten *why* the last one left?
Rebecca:	(*both eyes closed again*) Och that could have happened to anyone. She was far too sensitive that yin! (*Both eyes open*) Here, is it true she's still gettin' counsellin'?

← Effective use of humour

The door bell rings. Claire exits and returns, ushering in Amy who is clearly nervous about the situation.

Creative Drama script (single scene)	✓
stage directions	
action limited to one setting	
definite shape or structure	
few characters	
action takes place over a relatively short space of time	
limited number of plot 'events'	
lighting effects	
sound effects	
dialogue reveals characters' emotions, personalities, reactions, etc.	
climax or turning point in the action	
satisfying ending (thought-provoking for the audience?)	
spelling is consistently accurate	
punctuation is consistently accurate	
sentence construction is consistently accurate	
script could be performed	

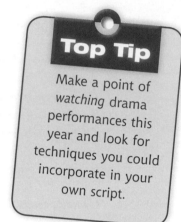

Top Tip

Make a point of *watching* drama performances this year and look for techniques you could incorporate in your own script.

Ideas for writing

If you are stuck for inspiration, have a look at the following suggestions. They just might provide you with the inspiration to kick-start your writing. Don't forget the importance of planning before you start!

Possible titles for short stories
- Interiors
- Homecoming
- The Life and Times of Alexandra Macleod
- A Much Travelled Man
- New Year's Resolutions
- The Anti-social Network
- Waves
- Where the Dogs Howl
- An Inescapable Truth
- Daylight Robbery!

- The Examination
- Soldiers
- Wha's Like Us?
- The Road to Nowhere

Possible opening lines for short stories

- John Smith caught, as he always did, the 7.58 to Paddington.
- I walk the line between our past and my present.
- Hergath watched the twin moons gradually appear above the horizon.
- She turned the key. Nothing. She turned the key again.
- The thrill of the chase is everything.
- I'm sitting at the same table in the same café at the same time of day. So far – no sign of him.
- The parcel on the doorstep was nothing special – just a slim cardboard box. What was inside, however, was anything but ordinary.
- Everyone disliked him. This was the simple truth. A simple truth in the same way that 'everyone has a father' is a simple truth – it could not be denied. He had long since stopped trying to deny it, even to himself.
- The adulation of the crowd had become essential to the girls. When they were on stage, nothing else mattered to them.
- 'Are we going to talk about this?'
  'What?'
  'You know fine what I mean.'

Top Tip

Keep a writer's notebook and jot down things you overhear on the bus, in your local coffee shop, at a party ... anything that you might incorporate in a story. Or keep the ideas as a memo or a recording on your phone.

Possible topics for argumentative or persuasive pieces

Remember that it is advisable to choose a topic or issue you are interested in or feel strongly about. Try to avoid topics such as *animal testing* or *abortion* or *size zero models* unless you feel passionately about them and feel you will be able to write effectively about them. It will make the task (and your writing) so much better if the reader gets a sense of *your* engagement with the issue. Remember your writing needs to show **depth and complexity of thought**.

- The Edinburgh Tram Project
- Scottish football referees should be awarded protected species status
- Online 'friends' can never replace 'real' friends
- Soap operas are a malign influence on our behaviour – we watch them at our peril
- Wind farms are destroying our landscape
- We should spend more money on transport systems
- Why every Scottish city should be a green city
- Schools should be more concerned with an individual's happiness than their academic achievement
- What role does the church have in today's society?
- What can we do to reduce the ever widening gulf between the rich and poor in our society?
- Do teenagers care about politics?
- Why is everyone so unpleasant to everyone else online?
- Computer gaming should be recognised for the complex entertainment art form it actually is
- Female teachers are more effective than male teachers
- Celebrities have forfeited their rights to privacy
- The world of the same. Why your town could be any town.

Possible scenarios for drama scripts

Always bear in mind that a script is *designed to be performed*.

- Two flatmates interview a third person to share with them
- A dramatic monologue by a bus driver
- A family gathering is disrupted by the revelation of a secret
- Two strangers at a bus stop get talking and discover something in common
- Three girls chat in a bar on a night out
- A family argues in the departure lounge of an airport
- A first date that goes wrong
- A dramatic monologue by an OAP
- A nervous employee is called into the boss's office
- A check out operator tries to make conversation with her customers
- A parent tries to give their teenage child some 'good advice'
- A passerby comes into contact with a beggar on the street
- Two football fans watch a game together and gradually reveal to the audience why they are addicted to their hobby
- A taxi driver overhears one side of a mobile phone conversation with unpredictable results
- A hill walking party gets lost and tensions within the group come to the surface

Ideas for personal reflective writing

It is difficult to suggest precise topics for personal reflective writing given the very *personal* nature of this kind of writing. You might like to think about the following possibilities:

- Reflect on your experiences as a young adult growing up in Scotland today
- Think about an object which means a lot to you and reflect on why it is important
- Think about how your personality has changed as you have grown older
- Reflect on your experience of education to date
- Reflect on your experience of love and relationships
- What are the most important things in your life and why?
- Reflect on what you feel is the single most important experience in your life to date
- Reflect on an experience which has changed the way you view the world
- Reflect on your perception of religion and/or spirituality
- Reflect on your experience of sport and/or competition

Literary Study

Introduction

In the English course, your study of Prose, Poetry, Drama and Media texts makes up the Literary Study Unit.

The language, structure and other techniques associated with these genres are tested in the Textual Analysis unit assessment. You will have to answer a number of questions which require close analysis of a piece of literature that you will not have seen before. These questions test your ability to understand, analyse and evaluate the text.

The Critical Essay paper in the external examination tests your knowledge of the texts you have studied in class.

This part of the book will look at:

how to study Prose Fiction
how to study Poetry
how to study Drama
how to study a Film
how to prepare for the Critical Essay paper

How to study Prose Fiction

When you read a novel or a short story as part of your Higher course you need to be able to do more than just offer an opinion on it (*'I really liked that'*, *'That was the dullest book I've ever read'*). You have to be able to analyse the techniques used by the writer in constructing the text and be able to say how effective you find them.

Structure

In some ways you are already an expert in this area. You've been hearing and reading and watching stories all your life. You already know how stories 'work'. You expect stories to have a beginning, a middle and an end. A more sophisticated description of this structure is as follows:

Exposition

The situation that exists at the start of the story. The reader is introduced to the characters, the setting is described and we are given an idea of what is going on. This is sometimes described as the 'equilibrium'.

Complication

Something happens to disturb the 'equilibrium' described at the start of the story and creates a problem for the central character(s).

Development

The 'chain of events' that takes place as characters attempt to deal with the problem.

Climax

The most exciting part of the story. Events come to a head.

Resolution

The strands of the plot are all worked out and a 'new equilibrium' is established.

A good number of the stories you will study will follow this pattern or 'classic narrative structure'. However, you need to be aware that a writer will sometimes play about with this structure in order to achieve particular effects. The writer might begin *in medias res*, in the middle of things, at some point in the development. This adds impact to the start of the story and will sometimes make it more dramatic. The writer might then use flashback to give the reader details of the exposition. The writer might not use any exposition at all until the end, leaving the reader to try to work out what is happening and why as the story goes along. There might be no resolution and the reader is left to ponder what happens next. Some modern writers have abandoned traditional structure entirely and leave you as the reader to create one as best you can as you read the 'story'.

Narrator

Ask yourself who is telling the story. Is it told by a character in the story in the **first person (I, me, we, us)**? If so, how does this affect our experience of reading the story? This technique might make us sympathise with the character as they become our 'representative' in the story – especially if they tell us their thoughts and feelings. Beware the **unreliable narrator** – a narrator who might not be telling us the truth or who might not know the truth of what is going on.

Is the story told in the **third person** – i.e. by someone who is not 'in' the story? If so it might be an **omniscient narrator** who can tell us everything that is going on and what all the characters are thinking. It might be a **limited narrator** who only tells us about a few characters and their actions and tells us much less about other characters and their actions. It might be a **demonstrative narrator** who only reports what characters *say* and *do* leaving the reader to work out the motives behind these actions.

Characterisation

It is very important to remember the simple truth that characters in novels and short stories are not real. It is not your job to treat them as if they are real people with all the hopes, fears, failings and neuroses that make up our personalities, even although the writer might present them to us in a very convincing way. What is important is for you to be able to analyse *how* the characters are created by the writer.

Characters can be created through what they say (the dialogue in the story) and what they do (their actions). Remember that nothing is in a story by accident. Everything means something. Look at this extract from the opening chapter of a novel by the Scottish writer, Andrew Greig. Notice how economically Greig introduces the characters of Murray and Tricia to the reader, through what they say and what they do. The extract is a good example of the **omniscient narrator** at work and you should notice how skilfully the writer suggests the characters' thoughts.

> Even in Kirkintilloch the sun was shining as Murray Hamilton eased the screws off the front licence plate on his old Kawasaki. His eleven-year-old sat on the steps of the council house with her guitar, hesitating between one chord and the next. His boy Jamie was kicking a football against the lean-to.
>
> 'So,' Tricia said, 'is this the end of a glittering political career?'
>
> He took the new plate from her and squinted into the light. Five years on the Council till he'd resigned, a thousand committee meetings, ten thousand doorsteps – and what had changed?

'Time to try anither way, Trish.'

The thread caught in the bolt and he began to tighten.

'You'll not be much of a dad in jail.'

He put down the spanner.

'I'll stop right now if you want me tae.'

Behind them Eve at last found the new chord and strummed it cautiously.

'I just said be careful. And don't get hurt.'

'Right darlin.'

Tricia began loosening the rear plate. She glanced at her husband's bowed head and for the first time saw that his tight red-gold hair was starting to thin around the crown, and the edge of his beard was touched with grey like the first touch of frost. Still, she grinned, as she put the screws down carefully beside her. Might as well be a bit daft before we're all past it.

Andrew Greig, *The Return of John MacNab*

When describing a character to the reader, sometimes the narrator will just tell the reader what a character is like.

John Rhodes, when he came, was big and fair … The face was slightly pockmarked. The eyes were pleasantly blue.

William McIlvanney, *Laidlaw*

But often the narrator's word choice or use of imagery will have *connotations* that the reader is expected to pick up on. What does the simile in the next extract suggest about John Rhodes?

'Hullo, you,' he said to Laidlaw and sat down across the table from them. 'Ye'll hiv a drink.'

'A whisky for me,' Laidlaw said. 'With water.'

'I won't bother, thank you,' Harkness said.

The blue eyes turned on him like a blowtorch lit but not yet shooting flame.

William McIlvanney, *Laidlaw*

Sentence structure

Don't forget to look for the effects created by the writer using sentences of different lengths and types. For example, the use of very long sentences with lots of punctuation might suggest things happening quickly or all at once. A series of short sentences might suggest rising tension or fear.

Mood

You should think of the *mood* of a piece of writing as the feeling or emotion or *atmosphere* the writer is trying to create in a piece of writing. Is it happy, gloomy, bleak, sympathetic ...? This can be achieved by reference to things like the weather (just think about the different moods suggested by a storm on an isolated moor and a morning of bright sunshine on a holiday beach) or to different colours (black has connotations very different to that of white).

Look at this extract from the opening of another of Andrew Greig's novels. By closely examining word choice, imagery and sentence structure see if you can spot *how* Greig creates a gloomy or downbeat mood.

A man on a motorbike finally came to the end of the road.

He sat astride contemplating gate, padlock, chain. Once he would have felt compelled to do something about those. Instead he switched off, unstrapped his helmet and let sound in.

Eight miles into the Rothiemurchus Forest, towards the end of a short winter's day, the world was quiet. No human voices, no birdsong, just a hiss of water from melting snow, damp wind seeping through the pines.

He got stiffly off the bike, clipped the helmet over the handlebars, climbed the gate and walked up the snowy path through the dark wood. He wore camouflage trousers and jacket but did not look like a soldier – at least, not from a war that anyone had won. After a hundred yards he paused, tossed the ignition key into the undergrowth and trudged on ...

... He took a smaller path and then a smaller one off that. At a ghostly intersection he stood in the rapidly fading light, pulled off his gloves and hurled one after the other into the darkness under the trees.

A while later, he unstrapped his watch, dropped it without breaking stride. He had no further need of time.

The last days had been a matter of discarding, in order, the remaining things that mattered to him. There was little left now. The pack was empty so he hung it dark and drooping on a branch, like a crow left by gamekeepers.

Andrew Greig, *Romanno Bridge*

Practice Textual Analysis

Many of the techniques you used for Close Reading can also be used for Textual Analysis (look again at the appropriate section of the Language Study Chapter).

Have a go at the following Textual Analysis exercise on Prose Fiction.

This passage is taken from the opening chapter of *The Sea*, a novel by John Banville. In it the narrator describes his return to a house by the seaside, many years after his encounter with the Grace family who came to holiday there.

THEY DEPARTED, the gods, on the day of the strange tide. All morning under a milky sky the waters in the bay had swelled and swelled, rising to unheard-of heights, the small waves creeping over parched sand that for years had known no wetting save for rain and lapping the very bases of the dunes. The rusted hulk of
5 the freighter that had run aground at the far end of the bay longer ago than any of us could remember must have thought it was being granted a relaunch. I would not swim again, after that day. The seabirds mewled and swooped, unnerved, it seemed, by the spectacle of that vast bowl of water bulging like a blister, lead-blue and malignantly agleam. They looked unnaturally white, that day, those birds. The
10 waves were depositing a fringe of soiled yellow foam along the waterline. No sail marred the high horizon. I would not swim, no, not ever again.

Someone has just walked over my grave. Someone.

The name of the house is the Cedars, as of old. A bristling clump of those trees, monkey-brown with a tarry reek, their trunks nightmarishly tangled, still grows at
15 the left side, facing across an untidy lawn to the big curved window of what used to be the living room but which Miss Vavasour prefers to call, in Landladyese, the lounge. The front door is at the opposite side, opening on to a square of oil-stained gravel behind the iron gate that is still painted green, though rust has reduced its struts to a tremulous filigree. I am amazed at how little has changed in the more
20 than fifty years that have gone by since I was last here. Amazed, and disappointed, I would go so far as to say appalled, for reasons that are obscure to me, since why should I desire change, I who have come back to live amidst the rubble of the past?

25 I wonder why the house was built like that, sideways-on, turning a pebble-dashed windowless white end-wall to the road; perhaps in former times, before the railway, the road ran in a different orientation altogether, passing directly in front of the front door, anything is possible. Miss V. is vague on dates but thinks a cottage was first put up here early in the last century, I mean the century before last, I am losing track of the millennia, and then was added on to haphazardly over the years. That would account for the jumbled look of the place, with small rooms giving on to bigger

30 ones, and windows facing blank walls, and low ceilings throughout. The pitchpine floors sound a nautical note, as does my spindle-backed swivel chair. I imagine an old seafarer dozing by the fire, landlubbered at last, and the winter gale rattling the window frames. Oh, to be him. To have been him.

When I was here all those years ago, in the time of the gods, the Cedars was a summer

35 house, for rent by the fortnight or the month. During all of June each year a rich doctor and his large, raucous family infested it – we did not like the doctor's loud-voiced children, they laughed at us and threw stones from behind the unbreachable barrier of the gate – and after them a mysterious middle-aged couple came, who spoke to no one, and grimly walked their sausage dog in silence at the same time

40 every morning down Station Road to the strand. August was the most interesting month at the Cedars, for us. The tenants then were different each year, people from England or the Continent, the odd pair of honeymooners whom we would try to spy on, and once even a fit-up troupe of itinerant theatre people who were putting on an afternoon show in the village's galvanised-tin cinema. And then, that year, came the

45 family Grace.

The first thing I saw of them was their motor car, parked on the gravel inside the gate. It was a low-slung, scarred and battered black model with beige leather seats and a big spoked polished wood steering wheel. Books with bleached and dog-eared covers were thrown carelessly on the shelf under the sportily raked back window,

50 and there was a touring map of France, much used. The front door of the house stood wide open, and I could hear voices inside, downstairs, and from upstairs the sound of bare feet running on floorboards and a girl laughing. I had paused by the gate, frankly eavesdropping, and now suddenly a man with a drink in his hand came out of the house. He was short and top-heavy, all shoulders and chest and big

55 round head, with close-cut, crinkled, glittering-black hair with flecks of premature grey in it and a pointed black beard likewise flecked. He wore a loose green shirt unbuttoned and khaki shorts and was barefoot. His skin was so deeply tanned by the sun it had a purplish sheen. Even his feet, I noticed, were brown on the insteps; the majority of fathers in my experience were fish-belly white below the collar-line.

60 He set his tumbler – ice-blue gin and ice cubes and a lemon slice – at a perilous angle on the roof of the car and opened the passenger door and leaned inside to rummage for something under the dashboard. In the unseen upstairs of the house the girl laughed again and gave a wild, warbling cry of mock-panic, and again there was the sound of scampering feet. They were playing chase, she and the voiceless other. The

65 man straightened and took his glass of gin from the roof and slammed the car door. Whatever it was he had been searching for he had not found. As he turned back to the house his eye caught mine and he winked. He did not do it in the way that adults usually did, at once arch and ingratiating. No, this was a comradely, a conspiratorial wink, masonic, almost, as if this moment that we, two strangers, adult and boy, had

70 shared, although outwardly without significance, without content, even, nevertheless had meaning. His eyes were an extraordinary pale transparent shade of blue. He went back inside then, already talking before he was through the door. 'Damned thing,' he said, 'seems to be. . .' and was gone. I lingered a moment, scanning the upstairs windows. No face appeared there.

75   That, then, was my first encounter with the Graces: the girl's voice coming down
      from on high, the running footsteps, and the man here below with the blue eyes
      giving me that wink, jaunty, intimate and faintly satanic.

1. Read lines 1–11. How does the narrator suggest the 'strange' or odd nature of the tide on
   the day that the 'gods' departed?   4

2. How does the writer signal a change of setting in time in the third paragraph
   (lines 13–33)?   2

3. What does the narrator mean by 'landladyese' (line 16)?   1

4. How effective do you find the use of the image '… amidst the rubble of the past' (line 22)?   2

5. Comment on the mood of lines 30–33 ('The pitchpine floors … been him').   3

6. How does the narrator's word choice and sentence structure in lines 34–45 help to
   convey his memories of the Cedars and the people who rented it 'all those years ago'?   4

7. What does the description of the Graces' motor car (lines 46–50) add to the reader's
   impression of the family?   3

8. What does the expression 'frankly eavesdropping' (line 53) tell us about the narrator?   1

9. How does the narrator convey a vivid picture of the man who comes out of the house
   in lines 53–59?   4

10. What do lines 60–74 add to our impression of the man?   3

11. How effective do you find the final paragraph (75–77) as a conclusion to this part
    of the story?   3

Check your answers on pages 81–83.   30

How to study Poetry

Introduction

When you are first faced with a poem you should approach the text by asking the following questions:

Understanding	What is the poem about?	*Look at the content, mood, attitude of the poet, subject or aspect of life revealed in the poem.*
Analysis	Who is speaking?	*The poet? Or has a persona been adopted? How do you know?*
Analysis	How is the poem structured?	*Regular structure or not? Look at stanza form, line length, rhyme, rhythm.*
Analysis	What other techniques have been used?	*Look at word choice, imagery (simile, metaphor, personification), sentence structure, sound.*
Evaluation	How effective are the poet's methods in conveying the meaning of the text to the reader?	*Think about your reaction to the poem as a piece of literature.*

Annotate your copy whenever possible. Mark it in any way that helps you to think about the text. There will be lines you find difficult to understand, but don't forget that the poem is not a 'puzzle' with only one 'solution' or 'right answer'. Ambiguity is an important concept in poetry – any poem might have more than one 'meaning'.

Here's a reminder of some of the technical terms you need to know:

Alliteration	Words beginning with the same consonant sound. It creates a pattern of sounds for a particular effect.
	Wee, sleekit, cowrin', tim'rous beastie, O, whit a panic's in thy breastie! Thou need na start awa sae hasty, Wi' bickering brattle! Robert Burns, *To a Mouse*
Association	Poems usually *suggest* more to the reader than they state. Poets want you to make associations based on the words on the page. Allusions, references, analogies, images, metaphors, similes all help you to employ associations.

Caesura	A pause within a line of poetry. Such pauses can break up the rhythm or meter of a poem.
	A thing of beauty is a joy forever: Its loveliness increases; it will never Pass into nothingness; but still will keep A bower quiet for us, and a sleep Full of sweet dreams, and health, and quiet breathing. John Keats, *Endymion*
Connotation	What the word *suggests* rather than what it simply *means* (denotation).
	e.g. 'sunset' means the time of day when the sun slips below the horizon (denotation)
	'sunset' might suggest ending, something drawing to a close, or even something like death (connotation).
Dramatic monologue	A poem in which an imaginary speaker addresses an imaginary audience. In *My Last Duchess* Robert Browning adopts the persona of the Duke of Ferrara negotiating terms prior to acquiring his latest wife. The poem reveals what happened to his previous one!
	That's my last Duchess painted on the wall, Looking as if she were alive. I call That piece a wonder, now: Frà Pandolf's hands Worked busily a day and there she stands. Robert Browning, *My Last Duchess*
Ellipsis	Missing out words from a sentence.
End-stopped line	A line of poetry that ends in a pause of some kind – indicated by appropriate punctuation.
Enjambment	Where the meaning, punctuation and sound of a poem do not stop at the end of a line but run on into the next. These two verses of a poem by Carol Ann Duffy show examples of both end-stopped lines and enjambment.
	I longed for Rome, home, someone else. When the Nazarene Entered Jerusalem, my maid and I crept out, Bored stiff, disguised, and joined the frenzied crowd, I tripped, clutched the bridle of an ass, looked up And there he was. His face? Ugly. Talented. He looked at me. I mean he looked at me. My God. His eyes were eyes to die for. Then he was gone, His rough men shouldering a pathway to the gates. Carol Ann Duffy, *Pilate's Wife*
Free verse	Poetry that has no regular rhyme or rhythm. Theme, images and layout are likely to provide a poem written in free verse with 'form'.
Imagery	Pictures in words. Poets use images to make us recreate imaginatively what is being described. See how economically Norman MacCaig does this in his poem, *February – not everywhere*.
	Such days, when trees run downwind, their arms stretched before them.

	Such days, when the sun's in a drawer and the drawer locked.
	When the meadow is dead, is a carpet, thin and shabby, with no pattern
	and at bus stops people retract into collars their faces like fists.
	And when, in a firelit room, mother looks at her four seasons, at her little boy,
	in the centre of everything, with still pools of shadows and a fire throwing flowers.
Inversion	Changing around (inverting) the usual or expected sequence of words in a sentence. It enables a poet to draw attention to a particular word or idea.
Lyric	A shorter poem which expresses the poet's thoughts and feelings.
Metaphor	The simplest way to think of this is comparison where one thing is described as being something else. Look again at *February – not everywhere* for some good examples.
Metre	Regular pattern of stressed and unstressed syllables in a poem.
Parody	A poem which imitates another for comic effect.
Persona	An identity assumed by the poet. Remember that the 'I' in the poem may not actually be the poet, it could be an entirely imaginary person. *Mrs Icarus* I'm not the first or the last to stand on a hillock, watching the man she married prove to the world he's a total, utter, absolute, Grade A pillock. Carol Ann Duffy
Rhyme	Words which have identical sounds usually at the ends of lines. The rhyme inevitably links the words rhymed and hence their meanings and associations. 'Half-rhyme' is rhyme which *almost* rhymes.
Rhyme scheme	The pattern of rhyme within a poem. Letters are used to indicate rhymes and non-rhymes with the first line of a poem being a, and the second a or b according to whether it rhymes with the first or not. Here are some familiar traditional rhyme schemes: The ballad : abcb The limerick : aabba The 'Habbie' Stanza often used by Burns : aaabab The Shakespearean Sonnet : abab cdcd efefgg Sonnet 130

My mistress' eyes are nothing like the sun;	a
Coral is far more red than her lips' red;	b
If snow be white, why then her breasts are dun;	a
If hairs be wires, black wires grow on her head.	b

	I have seen roses damask'd, red and white,	c
	But no such roses see I in her cheeks;	d
	And in some perfumes is there more delight	c
	Than in the breath that from my mistress reeks.	d
	I love to hear her speak, yet well I know	e
	That music hath a far more pleasing sound;	f
	I grant I never saw a goddess go;	e
	My mistress, when she walks, treads on the ground:	f
	And yet, by heaven, I think my love as rare	g
	As any she belied with false compare.	g
	William Shakespeare	
Rhythm	The sense of 'movement' conveyed by the arrangement of stressed and unstressed syllables. The rhythm in the following poem is very obvious – say it aloud and you'll notice the four stressed syllables (or beats) in the first and third lines of each verse and the three stressed syllables in the second and fourth lines. **A Slumber Did My Spirit Steal** A slumber did my spirit seal; I had no human fears: She seemed a thing that could not feel The touch of earthly years. No motion has she now, no force; She neither hears nor sees; Rolled round in earth's diurnal course, With rocks, and stones, and trees. William Wordsworth	
Simile	A comparison introduced by words such as 'like' or 'as'. Closed like confessionals, they thread Loud noons of cities, giving back None of the glances they absorb. Philip Larkin, *Ambulances*	
Stanza	Lines of poetry grouped together. Usually any pattern is repeated in following stanzas.	
Stress	Emphasis put on a syllable or a word.	
Symbol	Something which stands for or represents something. It is clear that 'The Sick Rose' by William Blake is not really a poem about a plant! Instead, Blake uses the symbol of the rose to stand for something innocent or beautiful which is being corrupted. O Rose, thou art sick. The invisible worm That flies in the night In the howling storm Has found out thy bed Of crimson joy, And his dark secret love Does thy life destroy.	
Theme	The central concern or idea behind a poem.	
Tone	The general mood of a poem and how the poet has signalled it to the reader.	

Practice Textual Analysis

In a Snug Room

He sips from his glass, thinking complacently

of the events of the day:

a flattering reference to him in the morning papers,

lunch with his cronies, a profitable deal

5   signed on the dotted line, a donation sent

to his favourite charity.

And he smiles,

thinking of the taxi coming

with his true love in it.

10   Everything's fine.

And Nemesis slips two bullets

into her gun

in case she misses with the first one.

Norman MacCaig

1. Comment on the poet's word choice in the title of this poem.   **1**

2. 'He sips from his glass' (line 1). How does the poet's language in the first stanza give you a clear impression of the sort of man 'He' seems to be?   **5**

3. How is the mood of self-satisfaction continued in the second stanza (lines 7–9)?   **2**

4. What does the poet gain from placing line 10 in a line on its own?   **2**

5. Comment on the effectiveness of the final three lines as a conclusion to the poem.   **3**

6. How effectively do you think the poem's form matches its content?   **2**

    15

How to study Drama

Introduction

The first thing to remember when analysing drama is that the text is something which has been created to be performed. Although a play has much in common with a novel in terms of characterisation, theme, etc, it is a very different kind of text, and the best critical essays will recognise this.

Stage directions will offer you vital information about how the play is to be presented to the audience. They will also provide you with an insight into the central concerns that the dramatist is exploring. If you are dealing with a play by Shakespeare, the stage directions will be minimal. In a modern play, they may be far more detailed, as the following examples from Arthur Miller's *All My Sons* show. The extracts are taken from the beginning of Act One.

The back yard of the Keller home in the outskirts of an American town. August of our era. The stage is hedged on right and left by tall, closely planted poplars which lend the yard a secluded atmosphere. Upstage is filled with the back of the house and its open, unroofed porch which extends into the yard some six feet. The house is two storeys high and has seven rooms. It would have cost perhaps fifteen thousand in the early twenties when it was built. Now it is nicely painted, looks tight and comfortable, and the yard is green with sod, here and there plants whose season is gone. At the right, beside the house, the entrance of the driveway can be seen, but the poplars cut off view of its continuation downstage. In the left corner, downstage, stands the four-foot-high stump of a slender apple tree whose upper trunk and branches lie toppled beside it, fruit still clinging to its branches.

These stage directions at once inform us of the setting in time and place ('an American town' suggests the universality of what will unfold). The apple tree reduced to a stump is an important *symbol* in the play.

Miller's stage directions also give us a very clear idea of the central character, Joe Keller, from the outset.

Keller is nearing sixty. A heavy man of stolid mind and build, a businessman these many years, but with the imprint of the machine-shop worker and boss still upon him. When he reads, when he speaks, when he listens, it is with the terrible concentration of the uneducated man for whom there is still wonder in many commonly known things. A man whose judgements must be dredged out of experience and a peasant-like common sense. A man among men.

Of course it is not only through stage directions that we learn about the characters. What they do (their actions), what they say, and how they interact with other characters all suggest to the audience how the dramatist intends us to regard them and you should pay close attention to all of these when you are studying the text. Look out for techniques such as *soliloquy*, when a character's innermost thoughts and feelings are revealed to the audience. In the following example, Shakespeare ensures the audience is made aware of Iago's plans:

Cassio's a proper man: let me see now;

To get his place and to plume up my will

In double knavery. How? How? Let's see.

After some time, to abuse Othello's ear

That he is too familiar with his wife;

He hath a person and a smooth dispose

To be suspected, framed to make women false.

The Moor is of a free and open nature,

That thinks men honest that but seem to be so,

And will as tenderly be led by th'nose

As asses are.

I have't. It is engendered. Hell and night

Must bring this monstrous birth to the world's light.

Othello I.3.386–398

Pay close attention to how a character develops and changes during the course of the play. Does your response to a character change as the action unfolds? Does the character match the definition of any common dramatic types, e.g. the *tragic hero*, whose downfall is the result of some flaw in their character?

Relationships will usually be at the heart of any play. Look at how the dramatist presents them to the audience and how they are used in the exploration of the central concerns of the play. Consider the use of *dialogue*. Is it *naturalistic* or are some speeches clearly meant to have *symbolic* significance? Look at how lighting and other staging techniques help to give prominence to some speeches. Find the lines which seem to encapsulate the central concerns of the play.

Look carefully at how the play is structured. The Ancient Greeks thought *tragedy* should follow the pattern: *exposition* (or introduction); *rising action* (or complication); *crisis* (some sort of turning point); *falling action* (showing the forces operating against the hero); *catastrophe* (usually the death of the tragic hero). However, not all tragedies fit neatly into this pattern. Many modern plays will have a much looser structure than the five acts of Shakespeare's tragedies, but you should still be able to spot *key scenes*, *turning points* and the *climax* of the action. Another technical term you should be able to use is *dénouement*. This refers to the part of the play when the outcome is revealed to the audience. How do you react to this?

Finally, consider what you think the dramatist's message is for the audience. What are the central concerns or themes of the play? How effective are the various dramatic techniques used in helping to convey these themes?

Practice Textual Analysis

This is an extract from *Long Day's Journey into Night* by the American dramatist, Eugene O'Neill. In the passage which follows, James Tyrone is spending time with his wife (Mary) and their two grown up sons (Jamie and Edmund).

EDMUND (*with sudden nervous exasperation*). Oh, for God's sake, Papa! If you're starting that stuff again, I'll beat it. (*He jumps up.*) I left my book upstairs, anyway. (*He goes to the front parlour, saying disgustedly:*) God, Papa, I should think you'd get sick of hearing yourself –

5   (*He disappears. Tyrone looks after him angrily.*)

MARY You mustn't mind Edmund, James. Remember he isn't well.

(*Edmund can be heard coughing as he goes upstairs.*)

(*She adds nervously.*) A summer cold makes anyone irritable.

JAMIE (*genuinely concerned*). It's not just a cold he's got. The Kid is damned sick.

10   (*His father gives him a sharp warning look but he doesn't see it.*)

MARY (*turns on him resentfully*). Why do you say that? It is just a cold! Anyone can tell that! You always imagine things!

TYRONE (*with another warning glance at Jamie – easily*). All Jamie meant was Edmund might have a touch of some thing else, too, which makes his cold worse.

15 **JAMIE**. Sure, Mama. That's all I meant.

TYRONE. Doctor Hardy thinks it might be a bit of malarial fever he caught when he was in the tropics. If it is, quinine will soon cure it.

MARY (*a look of contemptuous hostility flashes across her face*). Doctor Hardy! I wouldn't believe a thing he said, if he swore on a stack of Bibles! I know what 20   doctors are. They're all alike. Anything, they don't care what, to keep you coming to them. (*She stops short, overcome by a fit of acute self-consciousness as she catches their eyes fixed on her. Her hands jerk nervously to her hair. She forces a smile.*) What is it? What are you looking at? Is my hair –?

25 **TYRONE** (*puts his arm around her – with guilty heartiness, giving her a playful hug*). There's nothing wrong with your hair. The healthier and fatter you get, the vainer you be come. You'll soon spend half the day primping before the mirror.

MARY (*half reassured*). I really should have new glasses. My eyes are so bad now.

TYRONE (*with Irish blarney*). Your eyes are beautiful, and well you know it.

30 (*He gives her a kiss. Her face lights up with a charming, shy embarrassment. Suddenly and startlingly one sees in her face the girl she had once been, not a ghost of the dead, but still a living part of her.*)

MARY You mustn't be so silly, James. Right in front of Jamie!

TYRONE Oh, he's on to you, too. He knows this fuss about eyes and hair is only fishing for compliments. Eh, Jamie?

35 **JAMIE** (*his face has cleared, too, and there is an old boyish charm in his loving smile at his mother*). Yes. You can't kid us, Mama.

MARY (*laughs and an Irish lilt comes into her voice*). Go along with both of you! (*Then she speaks with a girlish gravity.*) But I did truly have beautiful hair once, didn't I, James?

40 **TYRONE**. The most beautiful in the world!

MARY It was a rare shade of reddish brown and so long it came down below my knees. You ought to remember it, too, Jamie. It wasn't until after Edmund was born that I had a single grey hair. Then it began to turn white. (*The girlishness fades from her face.*)

45 **TYRONE** (*quickly*). And that made it prettier than ever.

MARY (*again embarrassed and pleased*). Will you listen to your father, Jamie – after thirty-five years of marriage! He isn't a great actor for nothing, is he? What's come over you, James? Are you pouring coals of fire on my head for teasing you about snoring? Well then, I take it all back. It must have been only the foghorn I heard.
50 (*She laughs, and they laugh with her. Then size changes to a brisk businesslike air.*) But I can't stay with you any longer, even to hear compliments. I must see the cook about dinner and the day's marketing. (*She gets up and sighs with humorous exaggeration.*) Bridget is so lazy. And so sly. She begins telling me about her relatives so I can't get a word in edgeways and scold her. Well, I might as well get it over. (*She goes to the*
55 *back-parlour doorway, then turns, her face worried again.*) You mustn't make Edmund work on the grounds with you, James, remember. (*Again with the strange obstinate set to her face.*) Not that he isn't strong enough, but he'd perspire and he might catch more cold.

(*She disappears through the back parlour. Tyrone turns on Jamie condemningly.*)

60 **TYRONE** You're a fine lunkhead! Haven't you any sense? The one thing to avoid is saying anything that would get her more upset over Edmund.

JAMIE (*shrugging his shoulders*). All right. Have it your way. I think it's the wrong idea to let Mama go on kidding herself. It will only make the shock worse when she has to face it. Anyway, you can see she's deliberately fooling herself with that
65 summer-cold talk. She knows better.

TYRONE Knows? Nobody knows yet.

JAMIE Well, I do. I was with Edmund when he went to Doc Hardy on Monday. I heard him pull that touch of malaria stuff. He was stalling. That isn't what he thinks any more. You know it as well as I do. You talked to him when you went uptown yesterday, didn't you?

70

TYRONE He couldn't say anything for sure yet. He's to phone me today before Edmund goes to him.

JAMIE (*slowly*). He thinks it's consumption, doesn't he, Papa?

TYRONE (*reluctantly*). He said it might be.

75

JAMIE (*moved, his love for his brother coming out*). Poor kid! God damn it! (*He turns on his father accusingly.*) It might never have happened if you'd sent him to a real doctor when he first got sick.

TYRONE. What's the matter with Hardy? He's always been our doctor up here.

JAMIE. Everything's the matter with him! Even in this hick burg he's rated third class! He's a cheap old quack!

80

TYRONE. That's right! Run him down! Run down everybody! Everyone is a fake to you!

JAMIE (*contemptuously*). Hardy only charges a dollar. That's what makes you think he's a fine doctor!

85

TYRONE (*stung*). That's enough! You're not drunk now! There's no excuse – (*He controls himself – a bit defensively.*) If you mean I can't afford one of the fine society doctors who prey on the rich summer people –

JAMIE. Can't afford? You're one of the biggest property owners around here.

TYRONE. That doesn't mean I'm rich. It's all mortgaged –

90

JAMIE. Because you always buy more instead of paying off mortgages. If Edmund was a lousy acre of land you wanted, the sky would be the limit!

TYRONE That's a lie! And your sneers against Doctor Hardy are lies! He doesn't put on frills, or have an office in a fashionable location, or drive around in an expensive automobile. That's what you pay for with those other five-dollars-to-look-at-your-tongue fellows, not their skill.

95

JAMIE (*with a scornful shrug of his shoulders*). Oh, all right. I'm a fool to argue. You can't change the leopard's spots.

TYRONE (*with rising anger*). No, you can't. You've taught me that lesson only too well. I've lost all hope you will ever change yours. You dare tell me what I can afford? You've never known the value of a dollar and never will! You've never saved a dollar in your life! At the end of each season you're penniless! You've thrown your salary away every week on whores and whiskey!

100

JAMIE My salary! Christ!

105

TYRONE It's more than you're worth, and you couldn't get that if it wasn't for me. If you weren't my son, there isn't a manager in the business who would give you a part, your reputation stinks so. As it is, I have to humble my pride and beg for you, saying you've turned over a new leaf, although I know it's a lie!

JAMIE I never wanted to be an actor. You forced me on the stage.

110 **TYRONE** That's a lie! You made no effort to find any thing else to do. You left it to me to get you a job and I have no influence except in the theatre. Forced you! You never wanted to do anything except loaf in bar rooms! You'd have been content to sit back like a lazy lunk and sponge on me for the rest of your life! After all the money I'd wasted on your education, and all you did was get fired in disgrace from every 115 college you went to!

JAMIE Oh, for God's sake, don't drag up that ancient history!

TYRONE It's not ancient history that you have to come home every summer to live on me.

JAMIE I earn my board and lodging working on the grounds. It saves you hiring a man.

120 **TYRONE** Bah! You have to be driven to do even that much! (*His anger ebbs into a weary complaint.*) I wouldn't give a damn if you ever displayed the slightest sign of gratitude. The only thanks is to have you sneer at me for a dirty miser, sneer at my profession, sneer at every damned thing in the world – except yourself.

JAMIE (*wryly*) That's not true, Papa. You can't hear me talking to myself, that's all.

1. How do the stage directions and dialogue in lines 1–15 suggest a contrast between Mary and Jamie's views of Edmund's illness? 3

2. How does the dramatist suggest Mary's changing feelings in the speech beginning 'Doctor Hardy!' (line 18)? 3

3. How does the dramatist explore the contrast between the past and the present in lines 27–45? 3

4. Identify the 'mood' that is established by Mary's speech beginning 'It was a rare shade ...' (line 41) and show how this mood is established. 2

5. Explain the reason for the stage direction '(*quickly*)' in line 45. 1

6. What does Mary's long speech beginning 'Will you listen to your father ...' (line 46) suggest about

(*a*) her relationships within the family? 2

(*b*) her relationship with her housework and staff? 2

7. Comment on the style of language used in Tyrone's comment to Jamie 'You're a fine lunkhead!' (line 60). 1

8. Why do you think the dramatist has included the stage directions '(*slowly*)' and '(*reluctantly*)' in lines 73 and 74? 2

9. What are the contrasting emotions displayed by Jamie in lines 75–77? 2

10. How are the two different views of Dr Hardy conveyed to the audience in lines 78–87? 2

11. How does the language of lines 99–103 help to convey Tyrone's 'rising anger'? 3

12. How does the sentence structure of lines 121–123 help to reinforce Tyrone's 'weary complaint'? 2

13. What do Jamie's final words (line 124) suggest about his attitude towards himself? 2

30

Check your answers on pages 85–87.

How to study Film

Introduction

You might already know how to study media texts from your work at Standard Grade or Intermediate. If so, this section should serve as a useful reminder of the basic technical terms you need to be able to use in a critical essay. If you are coming to the study of film for the first time, then this should provide you with a brief introduction to the topic.

Studying a film is similar to studying a prose or drama text in many ways. The director of a film uses a range of techniques – just as a writer does – to create a narrative and so explore a central concern or theme. Concepts such as plot and characterisation are common to both film, and literature and you should not find it too difficult to comment on these aspects of the film you are studying.

It is likely that the film you are studying for the exam will follow the 'Classical Narrative' pattern of most 'mainstream' or commercial cinema releases. This means that the events in the film will follow a pattern of:

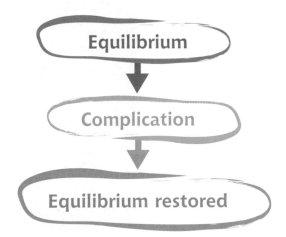

Equilibrium

↓

Complication

↓

Equilibrium restored

In fact, exactly the same sort of narrative structure that is explained at greater length in the section on *How to study Prose Fiction*.

If you think of any film you have been to see in the cinema recently, or watched on DVD, you should be able to match the story it tells to the structure outlined above.

Camera

When writing about a film, you need to be able to analyse the effect of the different camera shots and angles used by the director. Remember that nothing appears on screen by accident, *everything* is part of the director's 'art'.

Extreme long shot

Suitable for landscapes and aerial views.

Long shot

Suitable for framing characters in their surroundings (background will be more important than the characters).

Medium shot

Characters appear larger and dominate the screen. Useful for showing interaction between characters.

Close up

Used to highlight the significance of a character or object. A character's face might fill the screen to reveal a particular display of emotion. A director will sometimes use an *extreme close up*.

When a director uses a **low** camera angle it can suggest things like power or status (makes the subject seem larger).

A **high** angle (looking down on the subject) might suggest a character's lack of status or power. Always check from whose **point of view** we are seeing a shot.

A **straight on** angle keeps the audience in the role of onlookers, watching events unfold.

Look out for other techniques such as a **tracking** shot, in which the camera moves alongside characters, following their movements; **zooming** in or out; and **panning**, in which the camera stays in the same place and swivels to the left or right.

Top Tip

When analysing camera angles, watch the film with the sound turned off. This will allow you to concentrate on the camera work.

Mise-en-scène

This means everything that you see on the screen: **props, costume, lighting, special effects** – everything that has been 'placed on the stage' for you to view. Again, nothing is there by accident and you should be able to comment on the significance of all of these elements in the film. How are characters dressed? What are the connotations of the colours that we see? Are characters brightly lit or in shadow? What does this or that object symbolise?

Editing

A director chooses how the finished film appears to the audience by choosing how the various camera shots are joined together to construct the narrative. Usually a director will just **cut** from one shot to the next, but look out for when a **fade** in or out is used. **Montage** is the process whereby different shots are placed together to create particular effects (such as to suggest increasing fear or tension).

Sound

You also need to say something about the use of sound. **Music** is an obvious tool used by directors to create a particular mood. You should easily identify music that arouses emotions, such as sadness or excitement or apprehension in the audience. Don't forget to look at other sound techniques, such as **sound effects**. **Dialogue** spoken by characters and any voiceover also comes into this category. **Diegetic** sound refers to sound within the film itself (e.g. the sound of breaking glass when a character puts a brick through a window). **Non-diegetic** sound refers to sound that is 'outwith' the film (e.g. the music added to create particular moods).

Literary Study
Critical Essay

The Critical Essay paper can seem one of the most daunting things you have to do. Writing two essays, one after the other, without access to any texts or notes, can come as a bit of a shock. Especially if before there was the more comfortable world of drafting and redrafting critical responses at Standard Grade (perhaps with the added security of a detailed paragraph plan or writing frame provided for you). Nevertheless, you can improve your chances of success in this part of the exam.

The Critical Essay paper lasts for 90 minutes. You have to write **two** essays in that time. It is therefore very important that you get used to writing each essay in around 45 minutes.

There's no point in writing one reasonably good essay and then not having enough time left to complete a second one. **25** marks are allocated to each essay, and the paper provides **40%** of your overall grade.

Critical Essay paper

The paper itself is divided into five sections. These are presented in the same order each year: *Drama, Prose, Poetry, Film and TV Drama* and *Language*. You have to answer any **two** questions, but they must be selected from two different sections. The questions are designed to test your ability to *understand*, *analyse* and *evaluate* the literary texts you have studied. The essays also test your powers of *expression* and require you to be *sufficiently accurate* with your spelling, grammar and punctuation.

Let's consider each section of the paper in turn.

Drama

At the start of this section is a reminder of the dramatic techniques you should 'address' in your answer.

Answers to questions on drama should address relevantly the central concern(s)/theme(s) of the text and be supported by reference to appropriate dramatic techniques such as: conflict, characterisation, key scene(s), dialogue, climax, exposition, dénouement, structure, plot, setting, aspects of staging (such as lighting, music, stage set, stage directions …), soliloquy, monologue … (SQA English Higher Critical Essay 2010)

There are usually four essay questions to choose from. In recent years they have required answers on
- theme
- key scene
- characterisation
- relationship between characters
- situation
- staging/set/use of acting areas
- dialogue
- plot
- structure
- conflict
- turning point
- climax
- ending
- symbolism
- recurring motifs
- lighting.

Prose

This section is divided into fiction and non-fiction. The advice for **Prose Fiction** is as follows:

Answers to questions on prose fiction should address relevantly the central concern(s)/theme(s) of the text(s) and be supported by reference to appropriate techniques of prose fiction such as: characterisation, setting, key incident(s), narrative technique, symbolism, structure, climax, plot, atmosphere, dialogue, imagery ... (SQA English Higher Critical Essay 2010)

There are usually four or five questions on Prose Fiction. These are on the novel or short story. In recent years they have required answers on:

- plot
- opening
- ending
- characterisation/main characters/minor characters
- relationship between characters
- point of view
- setting
- narrative method
- narrative voice
- structure
- key incident or scene
- language
- theme.

There are usually three questions on **Prose Non-fiction**. If you attempt one of them you are told that:

Answers to questions on prose non-fiction should address relevantly the central concern(s)/theme(s) of the text and be supported by reference to appropriate techniques of prose non-fiction such as: ideas, use of evidence, selection of detail, point of view, stance, setting, anecdote, narrative voice, style, language, structure, organisation of material ... (SQA English Higher Critical Essay 2010)

Top Tip

Studying as wide a range of texts as possible during your course will increase your options in the exam and enable you to write about texts you have genuinely enjoyed.

In recent years they have required answers on:

- presentation of events in biography and autobiography
- structure
- description
- style
- use of humour
- insights given by travel writing
- the writer's stance.

Poetry

Any essay on poetry should:

... address relevantly the central concern(s)/theme(s) of the text(s) and be supported by reference to appropriate poetic techniques such as: imagery, verse form, structure, mood, tone, sound, rhythm, rhyme, characterisation, contrast, setting, symbolism, word choice ... (SQA English Higher Critical Essay 2010)

Sometimes a question will require you to write about **two** poems, either by the same poet or by different poets.

In recent years they have required answers on:

- theme
- situation
- structure

Top Tip

Remember you are not allowed to write an essay on *Prose Fiction* **and** one on *Prose Non-fiction*.

- sound
- rhythm and rhyme
- form
- imagery
- word choice/diction
- tone
- closing lines
- ambiguity
- mood/atmosphere
- emotion
- poet's or speaker's stance/perspective/personality
- location/setting.

Film and TV Drama

This section requires you to show your knowledge of media texts. *Don't* attempt a question from this section unless you have studied a media text as part of your course (however tempted you might be to 'analyse' that DVD you watched last night). Successful answers to questions from this part of the paper will:

… address relevantly the central concern(s)/theme(s) of the text(s) and be supported by reference to appropriate techniques of film and TV drama such as: key sequence(s), characterisation, conflict, structure, plot, dialogue, editing/ montage, sound/soundtrack, aspects of mise-en-scène (such as lighting, colour, use of camera, costume, props …), mood, setting, casting, exploitation of genre (SQA English Higher Critical Essay 2010)

Questions in this section require you to deal with concepts such as:
- characterisation
- music
- adaptation of novel or stage play
- setting
- atmosphere
- important sequence
- story/plot
- subject matter

Language

Only a very few candidates attempt a question from this section each year. Although the topics are very interesting, they require a specialist knowledge which is beyond the scope of this book.

The questions

If you look at any SQA past paper (or the specimen paper available on the SQA website) you will see that the questions for the Critical Essay tend to follow the same kind of pattern.

You are first asked to 'choose' a text. Remember, there are no 'set texts' at Higher. Each English Department in the country decides what to teach. But there is a statement which will help you to decide if the text you have studied is suitable to answer the question. After this comes what you have to do in the essay – often there will be two aspects to this.

Let's look at an example.

The initial statement: If the play you have studied does not contain a character like this you will not be able to produce a relevant response

Choose a play in which a central character experiences not only inner conflict but also conflict with one (or more than one) other character.

Explain the nature of both conflicts and discuss which one you consider to be more important in terms of character development and/or dramatic impact.

The first part of this task: It requires you to show your understanding of the text. This can sometimes be a reasonably straightforward aspect of the question.

(SQA 2010)

The second part of this task: This can often require a more 'sophisticated' response. An ability to 'evaluate' is required here.

Your essay must be a *relevant* response to the question. You must resist the temptation simply to write down everything you know about your chosen text. This is especially true when you are writing about poetry. You must avoid giving the examiner a 'guided tour' of the text, starting at the beginning and explaining all of the writer's techniques, even if that's how you were taught to analyse the poem in the first place. Although you do need to include enough *content* (in order to provide evidence of your understanding, analysis and evaluation), it is much better to write a shorter essay that is relevant, than a longer one which does not get to grips with the question itself. Taking five minutes to plan your essay and then 40 minutes to write it is a sensible way to allocate your time in the exam. It should help you to produce a well-constructed, thoughtful answer.

Writing the Critical Essay

Once you have chosen a text and identified the key words in the question, you should then spend some time on planning the essay.

Some people like to produce a mind map or spider diagram; others prefer a list of bullet points. It doesn't matter which method you choose, as long as you can do it quickly, and end up with the main points you are going to make.

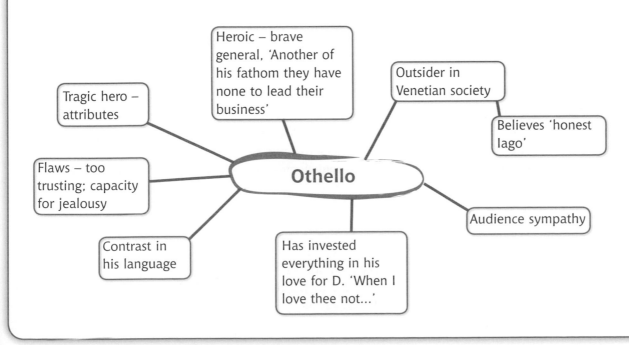

Literary Study

Taking five minutes to select a question and plan your essay should mean that you don't run out of steam after 20 minutes of frantic writing, wondering what to say next.

Let's look at an example of this in action. Look at the following Critical Essay question:

Choose a play in which the central character is heroic yet vulnerable.

Show how the dramatist makes you aware of both qualities and discuss how they affect your response to the character's fate in the play as a whole.

(SQA 2008)

Let's say you were going to use Othello as an example of a character who is 'heroic yet vulnerable'.

Here is a list of bullet points which would be your plan:

Othello

- Tragic hero
- Heroic – 'Another of his fathom they have none to lead their business'
- Vulnerable: flaws – too trusting; capacity for jealousy; lacks self-knowledge
- Outsider in Venetian society
- Believes 'honest Iago'
- Has invested everything in his love for D. ('when I love thee not ...')
- Audience sympathy
- Contrast in his language (poetic style v. echoes of Iago's use of imagery)
- Key scene: Act III sc. 3

Once you've decided on the points you are going to make, it's a good idea to *number* them so that the structure of your essay begins to take shape. You can then start to have an idea about how to *order* your arguments.

Once you have a clear idea of what you are going to write, you can begin. In the stress-filled environment of the examination room, it's a good idea to keep the structure of your essay as straightforward as you can.

The opening paragraph should:
- refer to the **title** of the text and its **author**
- refer to the **key words** of the question

The main part of your essay should then develop each of the points you want to make. It should develop in a logical way with a clear structure. You should pay particular attention to using **topic sentences** to signpost the stages of your argument and to refer back to the **key words** of the question.

The final paragraph should:
- refer back to the key words of the question
- bring your argument to a logical conclusion.

Remember, to produce an effective essay you must pay attention to **expression**. Your marker will check that 'structure, style and language ... are deployed to communicate meaning clearly and develop a line of thought'.

Top Tip

Don't forget that it *can* sometimes be useful to think in terms of some kind of a 'formula' for your writing. You might find it helpful to think in terms of **P**oint, **E**vidence, **E**xplanation (or something similar) when constructing your paragraphs. However, in the best essays such a structure isn't always that obvious to the reader!

Try using these expressions

The author/poet/dramatist/director	• attempts to … • develops … • demonstrates … • explores … • conveys … • exploits … • communicates … • attacks … • satirises … • utilises … • influences …
The author/poet/dramatist/director's	• aim here is to … • intention here is to … • purpose here is to … • intention here is to …
The author/poet/dramatist/director's	• skill is demonstrated by … • artistry • craft • mastery
Many critics	• consider that … • believe that … • have stated that … • have expressed the view that …
It is said that … It has often been said that … There can be little doubt that … This could be seen as the author's attempt at …	

Try using these to link your points

• similarly • likewise • in the same way	• although • for all that • however • on the contrary • otherwise • yet • but • even so	• to this end • for this reason • for this purpose
• accordingly • as a consequence • as a result • hence • therefore • thus • inevitably	• for example • for instance • in other words • by way of illustration	• as has been noted • finally • in brief • in short • on the whole • in other words

Using quotations

In order to meet the Performance Criteria for *Understanding*, *Analysis* and *Evaluation* (and so get a mark of at least 13/25), your critical essays must:

demonstrate 'secure understanding of key elements, central concerns and significant details of the text(s)'

and

explain 'accurately and in detail ways in which relevant aspects of structure/style/language contribute to meaning/effect/impact'

and

reveal 'clear engagement with the text(s) or aspects of the text(s) and stated or implied evaluation of effectiveness, substantiated by detailed and relevant evidence from the text(s) …' (SQA English Higher Critical Essay 2010).

Using quotations from the novel, play or poem that you are writing about will help you to show that you have sufficient knowledge of the text, and support your analysis and evaluation of it. But the quotations you choose to include in your essay must be relevant *and* support your line of argument. There is no point in learning ten quotations from, say, *Othello*, and then including them in your essay, if they are not relevant to the text specified by the question.

It is a good idea to keep a note of useful quotations for each text you study during the course. You can do it like this:

Act, scene and line no.	Quotation	Comment
I i 65	Iago: I am not what I am.	Iago's deceitful nature is evident.
I i 88–89	Iago: … an old black ram Is tupping your white ewe.	Iago's typically coarse and bestial imagery.
I i 115–116	Iago: … your daughter and the moor are now making the beast with Two backs.	See above.
I ii 63	Brabantio: … thou hast enchanted her;	Brabantio cannot believe that his daughter would choose to marry Othello.
I iii 76–93	Othello: Most potent … … I won his daughter.	*All of this speech*. Othello's typical dignified and highly poetic style. Note that he moves into prose under the stress of emotion and degradation (IV i 35–43; 169–211).
I iii 127–169	Othello: Her father loved me … … let her witness it.	*All of this speech*. Othello's account of his courtship of Desdemona. Again, take note of the highly poetic style.
I iii 291	Brabantio: She has deceived her Father, and may thee.	Brabantio's warning to Othello. An ominous hint of what Othello will later believe.
I iii 292	Othello: My life upon her faith. Honest Iago…	Ironic, given the later events of the play. The adjective 'honest' is applied to Iago throughout the play. The audience is always aware of the irony.

I iii 395–396	Iago: … Hell and night Must bring this monstrous birth to the world's light.	Iago's plot described as a monster; something unnatural.
II i 164–173	Iago: He takes her by the palm … With As little a web as this will I Ensnare as great a fly as Cassio.	Animal imagery again. Iago as the manipulator of events and people.
II i 278–279	Iago: The Moor, howbeit that I endure him not, Is of a constant, loving, noble nature,	Even Iago recognises Othello's nobility.
II i 285–287	Iago: For that I do suspect the lusty Moor Hath leaped into my seat. The thought whereof Doth like a poisonous mineral gnaw my inwards;	A possible motive for Iago's actions? A vivid image of what it is like to be jealous. Iago's twisted mind also suspects Cassio of sleeping with his wife (297).

Alternatively you can just annotate your text. Use any method that will make your revision easier.

When you are writing critical essays in the external exam at Higher, it's just you, a pen, a piece of paper and what's inside your head. So you must learn the quotations to use by heart. It's a good idea to keep them short (the exam isn't really a memory test, even though it can feel a bit like that sometimes).

If the quotation is a short one (a single word or short phrase), you can simply include it in the sentence you are writing (remembering to put it inside inverted commas).

For example:

> Othello's continual reference to his old comrade as 'honest Iago' is a good example of Shakespeare's use of irony in the play.

or

> Brabantio believes Othello has 'enchanted' Desdemona.

If the quotation is a longer one (a whole line or more from the text) you can do one of the following.

Add it to the end of your sentence:

> When confronted with what seems an ugly situation Othello commands everyone to
>
> 'Keep up your bright swords, for the dew will rust them'.

Place it, sandwiched, between the two parts of your sentence:

> Othello's command
>
> 'Keep up your bright swords, for the dew will rust them'
>
> shows his ability to defuse a potentially ugly situation.

Introduce the quotation with a verb of saying and a colon or comma:

> As MacCaig tells us,
>
> 'She lies
>
> in a white cave of forgetfulness.'

Longer quotations like the above should be placed on a new line for the sake of clarity in your essay.

Top Tip

Beware the dangers of 'micro-analysis' when writing about longer prose and drama texts. Questions about these usually require you to deal with the 'big issues' of characterisation, theme, setting, etc., and that is what you should concentrate on. Don't waste time, for example, discussing the significance of individual words in a particular sentence – your marker will not be impressed!

You will also see some writers simply using a colon to introduce a quotation.

For example:

> MacCaig is determined not to give in to his feelings:
>
>> 'I will not feel, I will not
>>
>> feel, until
>>
>> I have to.'

The danger with this last method is that it can make your essay seem rather staccato and disjointed, as the essay becomes simply one point after another, each followed by a quotation. You will find it difficult to construct any kind of fully developed, focused argument if you rely too much on this method.

The finished essay

Finally, let's look at how all of this is put together – from reading the question to the finished essay.

> Choose a **novel** in which one character generates hostility from one or more than one other character.
>
> Explain the nature of the hostility and go on to discuss how the novelist's use of it adds to your understanding of the novel as a whole.

We'll be using Robin Jenkins' novel, *The Cone-Gatherers*, as it is an appropriate text to use. You could use *any* novel you have studied *provided it matches the description in the first part of the question* (see the words highlighted in blue).

The key words of the question have been highlighted. Here's an example of the sort of notes you could produce to remind you of what to write:

First part of question
- Calum generates hostility from Duror (+ Lady Runcie Campbell)
- Description of Calum
- Why Duror hates him

  ➢ Personification of all that's wrong in his life
  ➢ Defiled his 'sanctuary'
  ➢ Revolted by anything misshapen or deformed
  ➢ Descent into madness
  ➢ Deer Drive (LRC's hostility toward Calum)
  ➢ Accusations against Calum
  ➢ End of novel – death of Calum

Second part of question:
- Theme of good v. evil
- Calum represents good and is sacrificed at the end
- Closing lines – LRC's moment of catharsis
- Jenkins' ending leaves the reader (like LRC) with hope

With these (brief) notes in front of you, you could then write something like this in the remaining 40 minutes or so you will have left.

In 'The Cone-Gatherers' by Robin Jenkins we see the character Calum generate hostility from the evil gamekeeper Duror.

> Opening paragraph identifies text and author and refers back to the question.

Jenkins makes the reader sympathise with Calum, a hunchback who is gathering cones with his brother in the woods of the Runcie-Campbell estate during the Second World War. Although he is deformed Jenkins portrays him as 'honest, generous and truly meek' and someone who is close to the world of nature. He is an expert climber and is 'as indigenous as squirrel or bird' in the trees on the estate. Jenkins effectively develops the character as someone who does not understand why there should be suffering in the world and throughout the novel he is portrayed as a 'Christ-like' figure.

> Quotations used to show knowledge of the text and to support the points made in the essay.

Calum generates hostility from Duror for many reasons. Duror 'hated and despised' the cone-gatherers and feels that they have defiled the wood which 'had always been his stronghold and sanctuary'. Through skilful characterisation, Jenkins portrays Duror's suffering. His wife has become hugely obese, their relationship has broken down and his attempts to sign up to fight in the war have been refused. Calum represents everything that is wrong in Duror's life. Jenkins tells us

> Topic sentence

'For many years his life had been stunted, misshapen, obscene and hideous; and this misbegotten creature was its personification.'

In addition to this Duror has always been revolted by anything misshapen or deformed and Jenkins even suggests that he sympathises with Hitler's treatment of 'idiots and cripples'. Duror is portrayed by Jenkins as a man descending into madness. He uses the image of a tree 'still showing green leaves' but with death 'creeping along the roots' to describe Duror and the reader is always aware of Duror's true nature and also that he is 'alone in his obsession'.

> 'Linking' expression

Duror uses Calum's unwilling involvement in the deer drive to try and remove him from the wood. Ironically it is at the deer drive that Duror's madness first shows in public when he kills the deer, confusing it with his wife Peggy. Calum attempts to save the deer but now also generates hostility from Lady Runcie Campbell who is annoyed that the event has become 'a shocking and demeaning spectacle'. Tulloch, a very 'moral' character, speaks up for the cone-gatherers. However, Duror's twisted mind also leads him to accuse Calum of exposing himself in the wood.

In the tense final chapter of the novel, the hostility Duror feels toward Calum leads to the killing of Calum and his own suicide.

Thus, Robin Jenkins uses this hostility to explore the theme of good versus evil and so adds to the reader's understanding of the novel as a whole. Calum's child-like goodness (a quality which he shares with Roderick) and his pity and concern for the animals of the wood make the reader sympathise with him. His 'sacrifice' at the end of the novel cleanses the

> Now the essay begins to deal with the second part of the question.

Literary Study

wood of evil and gives hope for the future. Jenkins again suggests a similarity to Jesus' death on the Cross as 'he hung in a twisted fashion' in the tree after Duror shoots him. The cones and blood which fall from him are another suggestion of this religious symbol.

After the two deaths (and Roderick's return to safety), Lady Runcie-Campbell undergoes a moment of catharsis and as she cries 'pity, and purified hope, and joy, welled up in her heart'. The reader experiences this too as we read this very powerful and thought-provoking climax to the novel.

Jenkins' ending leaves the reader (like Lady Runcie-Campbell) with hope. Although he allows the hostility between Calum and Duror to culminate in their deaths, evil is defeated even if at great human cost. As a result, the reader is left with a greater understanding of the theme of good versus evil and of the novel as a whole.

> Concluding paragraph refers back to the key words of the question.

This essay is 623 words long. You should be able to write something of similar length in the limited time available to you in the exam.

Preparing for the exam

It's likely you will study at least three genres in your Literary Study Unit, and you would be well advised to prepare at least one text from all three prior to the exam. You will only write about two of them, but you need the third as an 'insurance policy' (should the questions in one of your preferred sections not quite 'fit' your choice of texts). It is important to revise and prepare a number of different aspects of each text (see the features listed on pages 58 to 60).

You will also increase your chances of success by studying as wide a range of texts as time allows during your course. That way you will be able to write about something you have genuinely enjoyed reading or watching. The 'minimalist' approach of only studying say one poem and one short story and then practising essay after essay on them is unlikely to give you much of an insight into the study of literature. During your course you should (depending on the resources available in your school) be able to cover a novel, one or two short stories and/or some shorter pieces of prose fiction; a play or a film and a selection of poetry – although the number and variety of texts taught will be different from school to school.

Top Tip

It's a good idea to buy cheap copies of your longer texts for yourself – you'll easily find older second hand editions on sites such as *Amazon* and *Abebooks* – so you can annotate them in any way that will make your revision easier.

You must revisit and revise your texts throughout your course. You may finish looking at a novel in class in October, but don't leave it on the shelf until just before the exam. You must take responsibility for your own learning and keep updating your notes and knowledge throughout the year.

Look carefully at the feedback you get from your teacher on any practice essays that you do (especially those in a prelim) and try to avoid making the same mistakes in your next essays. However on no account should you learn an essay off by heart in the hope of using it in the exam – even if you got a good mark for it. The Critical Essay paper rewards your ability to think on the day of the exam, and it is highly unlikely that you will find a question that corresponds exactly with one you have done earlier in your course. Your teacher will probably show you exemplar essays as you prepare for the exam. They are to show you the principles of effective essay writing (structure, topic sentences, links between sections, use of evidence and quotation), but they are not designed to be memorised and reproduced on the day of the exam itself. The key thing to remember is to have enough things to say about the texts you have studied and then *select* from that body of knowledge in order to write a relevant response to the exam question.

Revising your texts for the Critical Essay paper

In order to revise your texts (drama, prose, poetry, film and TV drama) effectively for the exam you need to do more than just read them over and over again (although this in itself is no bad thing). You will, of course, be looking over the notes you made or were given during the course by your teacher and no doubt you will be doing any number of "practice essays".

One of the best ways to keep your revision more focused and relevant to the exam is by creating "Quality" cards for each of your chosen texts. These cards might be like the "cue cards" you perhaps used to deliver a Solo Talk as part of your Standard Grade course or they might be larger – you choose whatever size works for you. Many supermarkets now sell booklets of "Revision Cards" (usually in the run up to exam season) and you might find them suitable for this.

A "Quality" card is a way of storing appropriate notes on a particular feature or "quality" of a text.

One side of a card might look something like this:

Key points

"Quality" covered by card

Title of text: The Cone Gatherers Ending

What happens?
Lady Runcie Campbell runs to the cone-gatherers to ask for their help to rescue Roderick. Duror shoots Calum and then himself. LRC weeps at the base of the tree.

Function of the scene?
Culmination of the conflict good v. evil. Climax of the struggle between Dur. and the cone-gatherers. C is sacrificed to enable the estate to be cleansed of evil. Catharsis for LRC. Suggestion of hope for the future.

Literary techniques that add to impact?
Imagery: Dur. "So infinite a desolation" / "Christ-like" Calum

Important details and evidence in "shorthand" form

When you are creating your own "Quality" cards you need to make up a set of cards for each of the genres you might write about in the Critical Essay paper. It is a good idea to revise at least three of Drama, Prose, Poetry, Film and TV Drama.

Make up one card on each quality or feature you might be asked about in an essay question. Look at the features listed on pages 58-60 and start creating your own set of Quality Cards.

Make notes on your cards highlighting the key points about the feature or quality you have identified and the significant details (references to or quotations of examples of the quality) from the text which will support these points. These will help you create a relevant line of argument in your essay.

On the cards, use headings, sub-headings and bullet points or whichever "mind-mapping" techniques you are familiar with. You can use your own personal shorthand for the notes as long as you can understand it (you're not creating these cards for anyone else!) and can retrieve the information from the card even after several months.

The "cards" work equally well as documents on a laptop, tablet or smartphone. However you choose to make them, the most important thing to remember is that they should make your revision easier.

Top Tip

When practising Critical Essays, don't just choose the easy and obvious ones to go with the texts you are revising. Every so often pick an essay question at random from a selection of past papers or practice essays and force yourself to create a relevant response. You need to be able to deal with whatever the exam throws at you.

How the Critical Essay is marked

Your marker will judge your essay against the Performance Criteria. First of all your essay has to satisfy (or pass) all four criteria – if it doesn't, the highest mark it can get is 11/25. The Performance Criteria are as follows:

Understanding
As appropriate to task, the response demonstrates secure understanding of key elements, central concerns and significant details of the text(s).
Analysis
The response explains accurately and in detail ways in which relevant aspects of structure/style/language contribute to meaning/effect/impact.
Evaluation
The response reveals clear engagement with the text(s) or aspects of the text(s) and stated or implied evaluation of effectiveness, substantiated by detailed and relevant evidence for the text(s).
Expression
Structure, style and language, including use of appropriate critical terminology, are deployed to communicate meaning clearly and develop a line of thought which is sustainedly relevant to purpose; spelling, grammar and punctuation are sufficiently accurate.

The language of the Performance Criteria is sometimes not particularly 'user-friendly', so let's think about what these criteria actually mean.

- Demonstrating 'understanding … of central concerns … of the text' means you know more than just what happens in a novel or short story. You can show understanding of the **themes or ideas** the writer explores in the text. For example, show that the play *Othello* is not just about a general (who is tricked into believing his wife is unfaithful and who kills her and then himself), but being used by Shakespeare to explore the corrosive effects of jealousy and the very nature of evil itself.

- Explaining how 'relevant aspects of structure/style/language contribute to meaning/effect/impact' means you need to explain the various **techniques** used by the writer (remember, you are given a reminder of the sort of things to mention in the boxes at the start of each section of the question paper). These explanations should be used as evidence for the argument that you adopt for the question.

- If you choose to write about texts you have **genuinely enjoyed and/or found interesting**, then it will be easier for you to demonstrate 'clear engagement with the text' and say something about its effectiveness. Don't go 'over the top' in what you say about a text or writer! It always sounds artificial when candidates write things like '*Larkin's brilliant use of alliteration helps the reader to realise this*' or '*Jenkins' superb characterisation brings Calum to life.*'

- Even if your understanding and evaluation of your chosen text are competent, your writing (spelling, grammar, punctuation) needs to be 'sufficiently accurate' if your essay is to achieve a mark of at least 13/25. The examiners do accept that (unlike in your pieces for the writing folio where you have to be 'consistently accurate') you are writing in the stressful setting of the exam room with no opportunity to draft and redraft your essay. Nevertheless, you must do all you can to avoid common (and, at this level, very basic) mistakes such as:

  ➤ Comma splice – where you join ('splice') sentences together with commas rather than ending a sentence with a full stop and then starting a new one.

  ➤ Inconsistent spelling of common words – if you know you've got problems in this area make a word list as you go through the course and make learning these spellings a part of your revision routine.

  ➤ Using slang ('*Shakespeare uses well effective imagery …*'), colloquial language ('*Othello thinks Desdemona is cheating on him …*', 'text-speak' ('*The problem 4 Othello is …*'), abbreviations and symbols ('*Othello & Iago …*')

> ➤ Failure to organise your essay into paragraphs – the planning you do prior to starting the essay will give you a ready made paragraph plan.
> ➤ Incorrect use of apostrophes.
> ➤ Writing expressions such as *a lot* as one word.

Once your marker has decided whether or not your essay meets the Performance Criteria, he or she will then give it a category and a mark according to the following scale:

Category	Mark	Description
I	25	Outstanding
II	21 or 23	Very sound
III	17 or 19	Comfortably achieves the Performance Criteria
IV	13 or 15	Just succeeds in achieving the Performance Criteria
V	11 or 9	Fails to achieve one or more than one Performance Criterion and/or to achieve sufficient technical accuracy, or is simply too thin
VI	7 or 5	Serious shortcomings

(SQA Higher English Marking Instructions 2010)

Whether your essay gets the upper or lower mark in each category is down to how confidently the marker can place the essay in a category.

Some further advice

Short stories

Don't think that just because a short story is not as long as a novel it will be an easier text to study and write about in the exam. A well-crafted short story will make effective use of techniques specific to this genre and this can make it challenging to write about. Remember, you might be required to write about **two** short stories.

Non-fiction

If you want to prepare for a question from this part of the Prose section, you need to study texts such as essays (very different from *your* Critical Essays), travel writing, biography and autobiography, works on current affairs and politics, philosophy, etc. Remember that the techniques used by the writer in these kinds of texts are *different* from those used in prose fiction. (see page 59).

Poetry

The danger of the 'guided tour' has already been mentioned. You must avoid providing a line-by-line analysis of the poem. If your essay is no more than a series of quotations followed by comments, it will not 'address the central concerns of the text' and will not pass. Although you cannot offer an analysis of a poem without quoting from the text, you must make sure these quotations provide evidence to support your argument in your essay.

Film and TV Drama

Questions from this section should be dealt with just like those in the Drama, Prose and Poetry sections. You will need to be confident that you can make effective use of the appropriate technical terms (mise-en-scène; camera angles; sound; costume; ideology; lighting, etc.) to support your argument.

Practice Critical Essay questions

Try these against the clock (45 minutes).

Drama

1. Choose a play which made you reconsider your attitude to an important issue.
    Show how the dramatist introduces this issue and go on to discuss the effectiveness of the dramatic techniques employed to make you consider the issue in a new light.

2. Choose a play in which aspects of staging (lighting, music, set, stage directions ...) seem particularly important.
    Discuss how effective you find the use of these in the dramatist's exploration of the central concerns of the play.

3. Choose a play in which a central character is faced with a difficult choice.
    Briefly give an outline of the circumstances which lead up to this situation and go on to discuss how the dramatist makes you aware of the consequences of the character's decision.

Prose Fiction

4. Choose a **novel or short story** in which the style of writing greatly impressed you.
    Show how the writer's chosen style added to your understanding and appreciation of the central concerns of the text.

5. Choose a **novel** set in a location which is unfamiliar to you.
    Briefly describe the setting and go on to show how, despite the unfamiliarity, the novelist is able to make you consider themes which are universal.

6. Choose a **novel** in which a central character's death seems inevitable.
    Explain in detail how the novelist's portrayal of the character's death leads you to a greater understanding of the central concerns of the text.

7. Choose a **novel or short story** in which there is conflict between two characters.
    Briefly outline the nature of the conflict and go on to show how the writer uses it to develop a central concern of the text.

Prose Non-fiction

8. Choose a **non-fiction text** which seems to reveal a lot about the writer's point of view on a particular topic.
    Briefly describe what this point of view seems to be and go on to discuss in detail how this is revealed through his or her writing.

Poetry

9. Choose two poems which seem to have similar central concerns.
    Explain what the central concerns of both poems are and go on to discuss which poem you feel deals more effectively with them.

10. Choose a poem which you feel says something important to today's society.
    Discuss how effectively the poet's techniques help to convey this message.

11. Choose a poem in which you feel the content is enhanced by the poet's choice of a particular poetic form.
    Explain in detail how the choice of form adds to your understanding of the central concerns of the text.

Film and TV Drama

12. Choose a **film** or **TV drama** in which a character seems isolated from the rest of society.
    Discuss how effective you find the film or programme makers' representation of this character and go on to explain how this adds to your appreciation of the text as a whole.

Language Study: Close Reading

Answers on *When will English come to a full stop?*

1. **Locate and translate:** *1 mark for each of the following: the enormous number of words in the English language; English contains more than twice as many words as other major European languages.*
2. This is a **Meaning and Context** question. You would get 1 mark for giving the correct meaning: *Franglais is a mixture of French and English.* You would then get a second mark for reference to context: *French spellings/ borrowings of English words (le snacque barre; le hit parade).* A comment on 'Franglais' as a 'portmanteau' word might also gain you a mark.
3. **Locate and translate:** *English as a world language will have to give up its position of power.* (1)
4. A **Link** question. The four separate steps have been colour coded: 'difficulty of gazing into the linguistic crystal ball' refers back to the idea discussed in the previous paragraphs that it is difficult to predict the future form or status of languages; 'contemporary IT revolution' introduces the idea discussed in the following paragraphs that today's digital media are changing the ways in which we read and write.
5. **Locate and translate:** *So much change in the ways in which we read and write text* (1) *difficult to predict with certainty what sort of literature will be produced in the future.* (1)
6. **Locate and translate:** *IT alters how literature gets from the writer's mind to the reader* (1) *the reader works with a writer to produce the text.* (1)
7. **Locate and translate:** *Like literature, language must also change because of changes in (digital) technology* (1) *such changes are very difficult to forecast.* (1)

Answers on *Twilight*

See how many of the following features you spotted:

What you have instead in Meyer's work is a depressingly retrograde, deeply anti-feminist, borderline misogynistic novel that drains its heroine of life and vitality as surely as if a vampire had sunk his teeth into her and leaves her a bloodless cipher while the story happens around her. Edward tells her she is 'so interesting ... fascinating', but the reader looks in vain for his evidence.

List of three highly critical descriptions of the work ('depressingly retrograde ... borderline misogynistic')

Emotive word choice: 'depressingly'

Appropriate use of vampire image to reinforce the writer's opinion of the poor characterisation in the novel.

'bloodless cipher' image suggests the character is not portrayed as someone the reader can engage with

'looks in vain' suggests it's a hopeless task.

Alas, the only choice Bella gets to make is to sacrifice herself in ever-larger increments

'Alas ...' suggests Mangan's disappointment

'only choice' suggests the constraints placed on Bella

It sounds melodramatic and shrill to say that Bella and Edward's relationship is abusive, but as the story wears on it becomes increasingly hard to avoid the comparison

'melodramatic and shrill' shows Mangan acknowledges that some people might think she is going too far in her criticism. In the second half of the sentence she justifies this word choice.

Answers

To those less enamoured of Meyerworld

'those less enamoured' – a good example of understatement

'Meyerworld' seems dismissive – hints at a version of society that Mangan disagrees with

'The few signs of wit and independence' again highly critical of the character, suggesting there is little indication of the sort of qualities Mangan expects in a female central character

mute devotion suggests a passive, silent follower or disciple

slavish suggests Bella's lack of freedom in the relationship

Edward is no hero. Bella is no Buffy. Parallel sentence structures again underlining how Mangan feels *Twilight* suffers in comparison with *Buffy*. Short sentences add impact. Alliteration in the second sentence draws our eye to the sentence and reinforces the point being made.

And *Twilight*'s underlying message – that self-sacrifice makes you a worthy girlfriend, that men mustn't be excited beyond a certain point, that men with problems must be forgiven everything, that female passivity is a state to be encouraged – are no good to anyone. It should be staked through its black, black heart.

Parenthesis (inside paired dashes) is a list of what Mangan considers to be the negative message conveyed by the book and film. It's followed by the brief and blunt statement 'are no good to anyone'.

Final sentence contains another appropriate vampire image as Mangan suggests the *Twilight* phenomenon should be killed off in the same way a vampire is. Repetition of 'black' also serves to emphasise Mangan's (perhaps rather exaggerated) point that *Twilight* is almost something evil.

Answers on Practice Examination Paper (*Only a Theory*)

Passage 1

1.	Read lines 1–5.		
	(*a*) Explain why the writer thinks teaching Roman history and the Latin language is a 'big undertaking' (line 5).	3	U
	This is a straightforward 'understanding' type question so **locate** and then **translate** the appropriate words in the passage.		
	1 mark if you made the general point that it's because of the wide range **or** complexity of topics to be covered, and 1 mark each for any two of the following examples of that wide range: • poetry (the 'elegiacs' and 'odes' mentioned in the passage) • language structure ('grammar') • Roman conflicts or battles (you should be able to gloss 'wars' even if you've never heard or read the word 'Punic' before – remember you will encounter unfamiliar vocabulary in this exam) • Roman leaders (the 'Julius Caesar' reference) • luxurious and corrupt lives of rulers (a gloss of 'voluptuous excesses')		
	(*b*) According to the writer, what does this teaching require from the teacher?	1	U
	Another 'understanding' question. Locate the answer and translate it into your own words.		
	1 mark for a successful gloss of 'time, concentration, dedication', e.g. significant commitment/attention/focus/application/devotion.		

2.	Show how the writer's use of language in lines 6–11 conveys the threat posed by the 'ignoramuses' (line 7).	2	A

Remember that any reference to the writer's 'use of language' in a question should trigger a checklist of features and techniques to start running through your mind (*word choice, imagery, structure, tone, sound* ...). In a question like this you can score 2 marks for an 'insightful' or well-expressed point about a single feature. What makes a comment 'insightful'? It's all to do with how perceptive your understanding of the technique the writer is using seems to be and how well you express any comment about it. It's always safer to make more than one point in a 2 mark question! Half marks are still used in the marking of Analysis questions in the exam. As in all Analysis type questions you need to refer to (and quote) an appropriate feature or technique and then comment on it.

For this question you can score up to 2 marks for a single well-expressed point. 1 mark for each more basic point. A 'reference alone' (just pointing out a feature or technique without a comment) does not score any marks (0). Each of the possible answers set out below consists of a reference and then a suggested comment.

Imagery (remember to explain the 'root' of the image in your answer)
*   baying pack hounds   chasing their quarry
*   preyed upon   predators attacking weaker animals

Word choice
*   baying   loud/menacing
*   ignoramuses   anti-intellectual/uncivilised
*   scurry about   animal like/unattractive/secretive/busybodies
*   tirelessly   never giving up

Sound
*   alliteration   'precious', 'preyed' catches the eye (or ear) and helps to underline the point the writer is making

3.	Why does the writer include the list of languages in lines 12–13?	2	U

The best answer to give would be:

As evidence (of evolution) to highlight his point that it's ridiculous such a large number of (related) languages would suddenly exist.

This would score (2).

If you only made a more basic point, along the lines of:

It shows the number of languages influenced by Latin/suggests the relevance of teaching Latin given its influence on modern languages.

You would score (1).

4.	Referring to specific language features, how effective do you find lines 15–18 as a conclusion to the opening paragraph?	4	A/E

In answering a question like this you need to make sure that the features you identify and comment on relate back to what has gone before in the paragraph.

Up to 2 marks for a sophisticated analysis of any one feature. 1 mark for a more basic point. For full marks structure *and* word choice must be covered.

Possible answers:

Sentence structure
*   balanced structure ('Instead of devoting ... , you are forced to ...') highlights time wasted on answering attacks
*   colon introduces expansion of the idea of the 'rearguard defence'

Word choice
- 'noble vocation'   higher calling/emphasises status of the Latin teacher
- 'rearguard defence'   desperately fighting off attackers
- 'make you weep'   suggests sense of despair engendered by ignorant attacks
- 'exhibition'   shows their lack of self-awareness/sense of proportion
- 'ignorant'   sums up critics' lack of knowledge
- 'prejudice'   unthinking response/base instinct

Tone
- You could also make the point that the tone of these lines (one of anger, despair or exasperation at the 'ignoramuses') is in keeping with the rest of the paragraph and support it with reference to any of the language features outlined above.

5.	Explain the characteristics of the 'Holocaust-deniers' (line 22) as described by the writer.	2	U
	This is another **locate and translate** question.		
	1 mark each for a successful gloss of any two of		
	• 'vocal' promote their message (not just 'loud') • 'superficially plausible' believable on a very simplistic level • 'adept at seeming learned' skilled at appearing intellectual/academic		
6.	Show how the writer's language makes clear his disapproval of the situation faced by the hypothetical history teacher in lines 26–32.	4	A
	This is another question where the words 'writer's language' should trigger that checklist of features and techniques in your mind. Below are possible comments you could make on word choice, punctuation and structure.		
	You would score up to 2 marks for a sophisticated analysis of any one feature. 1 mark for a more basic point. For full marks **two** language features must be covered. • 'continually faced with' incessant nature of problem • 'belligerent' aggressive • inverted commas around 'equal time' highlight the writer's feeling that this is a waste of time • inverted commas around 'teach the controversy' and 'alternative theory' suggest the lack of status he awards these ideas • inverted commas around 'respected' highlight his own lack of respect for the idea • 'Fashionably relativist' trendy/lacking certainty/clarity • 'chime in' irritating addition to the debate • colon and semi-colon used to structure the relativist intellectuals' argument that 'all points of view are equally valid'		
7.	Referring to specific words and/or phrases, show how the sentence 'The plight … dire' (line 33) performs a linking function in the writer's argument.	2	U
	Remember the formula to answer this kind of question: quote and comment on the words which refer back to the *previous* part of the passage and then quote and comment on the words which introduce the *next* part of the writer's argument. Remember there are also often marks to be gained by commenting on linking words such as 'but', 'yet', etc.		
	You would get 1 mark for each of the following: • 'not less dire' is a reference back to the problematic situations faced by the hypothetical teachers mentioned in previous paragraphs • 'plight of science teachers today' introduces the description of the situation faced by science teachers at present		

8.	Read lines 33–43.		

8. Read lines 33–43.

Show how the writer's use of language in this paragraph highlights his feelings of sympathy for science teachers today. You should refer to at least two features (word choice, sentence structure, imagery …) in your answer. — **4** **A**

This question helpfully reminds you of the sort of language features to comment on.

Up to 2 marks for a sophisticated analysis of any one feature. 1 mark for a more basic point. For full marks **two** language features must be covered.

Possible answers:

Structure
- repetition of 'When they … when they … when they …' shows extent of their efforts
- list of good they do separated by semi-colons
- balanced structure of second sentence in the paragraph (contrast between positive efforts followed by description of obstacles)
- repeated structures with contrasting meanings: 'explore and explain'/'harried and stymied'/'hassled and bullied'
- repetition of 'They are …' suggests the variety of difficulties faced
- contrast – 'Once … now …'

Word choice
- 'honestly' — shows their integrity
- 'very nature of life itself' — dealing with fundamental issues
- 'harried' — chased
- 'stymied' — obstructed/blocked
- 'hassled' — bothered
- 'bullied/threatened/menacing' — putting pressure on the teacher
- 'wasted at every turn' — consistently interfered with
- 'sarcastic smirks' — negative attitude of pupils/belittling teacher's efforts
- 'close-folded arms' — body language mirrors 'closed' minds
- 'brainwashed' — as if indoctrinated/conditioned
- 'state-approved' — big-brother society
- 'systematically expunged' — methodically/deliberately removed from the textbooks
- 'bowdlerized' — altered from the original/loss of original sense or true meaning

Punctuation
- Inverted commas around 'change over time' suggests it is a less precise expression than 'evolution'.

OR
- Inverted commas are used simply because he is quoting from a 'politically-correct' textbook and wishes the reader to share his outrage at the use of the term.

9. Read lines 44–57.

(a) According to the writer, why is his book not 'anti-religious' (line 48)? — **1** **U**

It's a U question so you must use your own words. Possible answers:

He has already written one on that theme and that is not the purpose of this one.

OR

He feels he's already met that challenge (reference to got the T-shirt).

Answers

	(b) How effective do you find the image 'cranked the universe up' (lines 53–54) in the context of the passage as a whole?	2	A/E
	Remember to explain the 'root' of this image – say what is being compared to what. Make sure you justify why you think it is effective (or not).		
	2 marks for an insightful comment. 1 mark for a more basic response.		
	Creating the universe is compared to starting an engine (which runs by itself thereafter). 'Cranked' doesn't sound like a particularly 'high-tech' piece of engineering. It is effective because the image allows the writer to poke (gentle) fun at those who hold such beliefs. This lends weight to the author's own theory.		
10.	How does the writer's use of sentence structure in the final paragraph emphasise his position on this subject?	2	A
	Look carefully at the final paragraph. What aspects of structure did you spot?		
	Up to 2 marks for an insightful comment on one feature. 1 mark for a more basic comment.		
	Possible answers: • short, blunt first sentence states case clearly • repetition of 'Beyond ... beyond ...' shows the extent of the case for evolution/ irrefutable quality of the evidence • 'beyond sane, informed, intelligent doubt' – triad of adjectives effectively shows the quality of the evidence for his argument • repetition of 'fact' to drive home the certainty he has • repetition of 'cousins ...' to emphasise the inter-related nature of all species • 'somewhat more distant ... more distant ... still ... yet more distant ...' suggests the breadth of the evolutionary process • cumulative effect of 'not self-evidently, tautologically, obviously true' • final sentence ends with simple statement reinforcing his case		
		(29)	

Answers on Practice Examination Paper

Remember when answering **U** (**Understanding**) questions you should always use your own words as much as you can.

11.	Read lines 1–10.		
	(a) Explain the question posed by the writer in line 1.	1	U
	A straightforward question to get you started on the second passage. All you have to do is put the question into your own words, particularly the word 'creationists'.		
	1 mark for appropriate gloss, e.g. How do teachers deal with pupils who do not believe in evolution/have strong religious beliefs?		
	Obviously, if you just write down the words used by the writer, you score 0.		
	(b) Show how the writer's use of contrast makes his argument clear in lines 2–10.	3	A
	Remember to give both sides of any contrast to illustrate your answer.		
	1 mark for the point that he sides with science.		
	1 mark each for any two of the following examples of contrast: • 'overwhelming majority' v. '(only) 10%'		

	• 'biologists'/'scientists' v. 'people' • 'universe ... 13 to 14 billion years old' v. 'Earth ... some 10,000 years old' (seems ridiculously young) • reference to 'single coherent discipline'/'conceptual framework' v. reference to 'the Bible or the Qur'an'		
12.	Read lines 11–15. **Explain the connection between 'Evolution and cosmology' and religion.** 1 mark for gloss of 'they can be seen ... Muslim Scriptures', e.g. *they seem to give an account of how life and the cosmos began which opposes that claimed by the major religions of the world.* You might have given a more 'condensed' gloss along the lines of *Both evolution and cosmology go against religion* and this would also get a mark.	1	U
13.	Read lines 21–28. **Explain the fear of 'Many scientists, and some science educators'.** Another chance for you to **Find** and **Replace with ...** 1 mark for appropriate gloss, e.g. *asking pupils to think about 'non-scientific' theories about the origins of life awards status to these ideas* OR *if dubious topics are included in science lessons people will think they are true.*	1	U
14.	Read lines 29–38. **How effective do you find the writer's reference to his own experience as a learner as a piece of evidence to support his argument?** 1 mark for the general point that creationism can be discussed in schools. 2 further marks for any two of the following: • parenthetical comment 'and taught it extremely well in my view', suggests high quality of teaching/positive experience • 'so exciting' suggests pupils' positive response to opportunities to debate things openly • 'discuss almost anything' suggests no subject off-limits • 'defend our thinking' suggests not just unsubstantiated beliefs • 'logical argument' suggests use of reason	3	A/E
15.	Read lines 39–42. **According to the writer, when might it be 'appropriate to deal with the issue' in class?** 1 mark for an appropriate gloss, e.g. *how relaxed the teacher is in exploring the topic and what the pupils in the class are like.* 0 if you didn't use your own words!	1	U
16.	**How does the writer's use of language in lines 39–45 make his own opinions clear to the reader?** Structure, word choice and tone are all things you could comment on in response to this question. Up to 2 marks for a single insightful comment. 1 mark for each more basic point. For full marks at least two language features should be covered. Structure • balanced/parallel structure around semi-colon 'Some students ...; others ...' • balanced statements '... I don't believe ... I do believe ...' • dash (line 49) introduces expansion of the point – the additional benefit of such an approach	4	A

Answers

	Word choice • 'very heated' worked up/annoyed • 'silent' opt out of the debate • 'seriously and respectfully' illustrates he does not approach this frivolously Tone • undogmatic/reasonable 'Having said that ...'; 'While it is unlikely ...'		
17.	How effective do you find the final paragraph as a conclusion to the passage? In answering this type of question you will usually find it easier to argue that it *is* effective and supply evidence to support your claim. Up to 2 marks for an insightful response. 1 mark for a more basic point. • ends with statement on how to make good use ('profitably') of what others see just as a mistake ('simple misconception') • reasonable tone continues in the writer's final acceptance of the limits of education in changing people's view of the world ('however well taught')	2	E
		(16)	

Question on both passages

18.	Which passage do you think offers the more thought provoking ideas about the teaching of evolution and creationism? Justify your choice by referring to the **ideas** and **style** of both passages. The SQA marking instructions for these kinds of questions tend to be as follows: *5 marks – clear and intelligent understanding of both passages; evaluative comment is thoughtful and convincing* *4 marks – clear understanding of both passages; evaluative comment is reasonably convincing* *3 marks – understanding of both passages; there is some evaluative comment* *2 marks – some understanding of both passages; at least one appropriate evaluative comment* *1 mark – one or two relevant but unconvincing comments'* (SQA Close Reading Marking Instructions 2010) Mention could be made of the following: Passage 1 Ideas • Use of two extended analogies – Latin teacher, History teacher – to show the difficulties posed by those with opposing ideas • Problems facing science teachers teaching evolution • 'American' problem now present in Europe • Acceptance of evolution by some theologians • Very strong closing statement of the case for evolution Style • Clear sense of a personal stance • Very one-sided throughout • Use of rhetorical devices including lists, repetition, triads – all of which contribute to the highly emphatic tone • Emotive use of Holocaust reference	5	U/E

Passage 2

Ideas

*   Also deals with problems facing science teachers and the teaching of evolution
*   Conflicting 'world views' – creationist v. scientific
*   Reference to American textbook
*   Reference to the writer's own experience of being taught science
*   The need to encourage open debate in the science classroom

---

*   The teaching of science can benefit from considering creationist ideas
*   Acceptance by the writer that he will not change anyone's mind in the short term

Style

*   Also a very *personal* statement of the issue
*   Much more balanced/neutral in terms of tone when compared with Passage 1 ('... there is much to be said for ...'; 'I agree with the first sentence but disagree with the second.'; 'Having said that ...'; '... not as a misconception but as a world view'; 'While it is unlikely ...)
*   Clear statements without recourse to imagery or emotive language

		(5)	
Total		**(50)**	

Answers

Literary Study: Prose fiction

Answers on *The Sea*

1.	Read lines 1–11. How does the narrator suggest the 'strange' or odd nature of the tide on the day that the 'gods' departed?	4
	To answer this question you should look for examples of the writer's word choice, imagery and other language features. You could mention	
	• the repetition of 'swelled and swelled'	
	• the use of the phrases 'unheard-of heights' and 'longer ago than any of us could remember' suggest that a tide this high was outwith the experience of the locals	
	• 'parched' suggests the (usually) extreme dryness of the sand	
	• personification of the boat ('must have thought it was being granted a relaunch') to emphasise the unusual nature of the event	
	• seabirds 'unnerved' and 'unnaturally white'	
	• simile 'bulging like a blister' suggests something rising up and covering what's underneath (an unattractive image)	
	• word choice 'malignantly agleam' suggests something diseased or deadly	
	Award yourself 1 mark for each feature you commented on.	
2.	How does the writer signal a change of setting in time in the third paragraph (lines 13–33)?	2
	1 mark each for the following:	
	• verb tense in the opening paragraph has changed from past 'departed'; 'mewled'; 'looked', etc., to present ('name is ... the Cedars'; '... which Miss Vavasour prefers to call', etc.)	
	• You should also have noticed references such as '... clump of those trees ... still grows' and 'I am amazed at how little has changed' which signal to the reader that this part of the narrative is set in the present	
3.	What does the narrator mean by 'landladyese' (line 16)?	1
	An answer which suggests that 'landladyese' is vocabulary used by landladies to describe the rooms in a boarding house – presumably to make them sound more attractive or 'refined' (e.g. 'lounge' instead of 'living room') would gain 1 mark.	
4.	How effective do you find the use of the image '... amidst the rubble of the past' (line 22)?	2
	In answering questions like these, it is almost always easier to say that an image *is* effective and go on to say why. You are always free to say that an image is not particularly effective as long as you justify your answer with reference to the text.	
	This image does seem effective because the metaphor suggests *both* the physical effects of the passing of time – things deteriorate and crumble just as the struts in lines 18–19 have been eaten away by rust – *and* the idea that there was some kind of difficult or harmful or destructive episode in the narrator's past that he has come to relive by coming back to the Cedars. You might also have suggested that 'rubble' is an appropriate way to describe memories which are confused and not 'clear-cut' ('jumbled' and 'haphazardly' continue this idea later on in the paragraph).	
	A 'full' answer would gain 2 marks. 1 mark for a more basic explanation.	

5.	Comment on the mood of lines 30–33 ('The pitchpine floors … been him').	3
	Remember that the 'mood' of a piece of writing relates to the emotional attitude taken to the subject by a writer. Here the mood seems *wistful* or *yearning* – the narrator seems to be wishing for a life he has not had ('Oh, to be him. To have been him'). The description of the things which lend the rooms a 'nautical note' (reminding the narrator of things to do with sailing) help to create this tone. The 'pitchpine floors' suggest the deck of a ship; the 'spindle-backed chair' is typical of what you would find in the captain's cabin of an old sailing ship. The narrator conjures up a romanticised (you might say clichéd) image of 'an old seafarer', 'landlubbered at last' 'dozing' while the winter gale rattles the window frames.	
	1 mark for correctly identifying the mood ('wistful'; 'yearning' **or similar** – don't worry if you have expressed it slightly differently) and 1 mark for each reference plus comment on a feature of the text. As always, it is the quality of your comment that is crucial.	
6.	How does the narrator's word choice and sentence structure in lines 34–45 help to convey his memories of the Cedars and the people who rented it 'all those years ago'?	4
	You should have spotted the following:	
	Word choice	
	• 'infested' suggests it was overrun as if by pests of some kind	
	• 'mysterious' suggests he was intrigued by the couple	
	• 'grimly walked their sausage dog in silence' conveys a vivid (comic?) picture of the couple	
	Sentence structure	
	• parenthesis in lines 36–38 gives additional information about the hostility of the doctor's children	
	• list of tenants in lines 41–44 suggests the wide variety of people who rented the house	
	• short final sentence signals the significance of the arrival of the Grace family to the narrator (the 'gods' of the story)	
	1 mark for each relevant point made. You need to have mentioned both word choice and sentence structure to gain full marks.	
7.	What does the description of the Graces' motor car (lines 46–50) add to the reader's impression of the family?	3
	Any three of the following for 1 mark each:	
	• 'scarred and battered' suggests it's seen a lot of use; that they've travelled widely	
	• 'beige leather seats' and the 'polished wood' steering wheel hint at an expensive model suggesting the family is well off (or perhaps *were* well off as it is now 'scarred and battered')	
	• 'low-slung' and 'sportily raked' suggest the glamour of a fast car and so makes its owners seem glamorous	
	• the 'touring map of France, much used' suggests foreign trips and adds to the family's exotic appeal	
	• the books 'thrown carelessly on the shelf' perhaps suggest the family's relaxed attitude to life	
8.	What does the expression 'frankly eavesdropping' (line 53) tell us about the narrator?	1
	1 mark for saying that it tells us he admits ('frankly') he was listening in to the sounds coming from the house.	

9.	How does the narrator convey a vivid picture of the man who comes out of the house in lines 53–59? You could comment on any of the following for 1 mark each: • the impression of physical strength ('short … all shoulders and chest') • exotic appearance ('crinkled, glittering-black hair'; 'skin was so deeply tanned by the sun it had a purplish sheen'; 'pointed black beard'; 'Even his feet …') • seems older than he is ('flecks of premature grey') • relaxed ('loose green shirt unbuttoned and khaki shorts and was barefoot') • he is an obvious contrast to the 'majority of fathers' who 'were fish-belly white below the collar-line'	4
10.	What do lines 60–74 add to our impression of the man? You could mention any three of the following: • setting his tumbler at a 'perilous angle' on the roof of the car confirms our impression of him as someone with a carefree attitude towards life • 'slammed' hints at a display of anger or frustration; suggests his volatility • 'a comradely, a conspiratorial wink' suggests he treats the narrator as an equal; he doesn't behave like the other adults in the boy's life • 'masonic' suggests the wink is a kind of secret signal between the man and boy	3
11.	How effective do you find the final paragraph (lines 75–77) as a conclusion to this part of the story? Here are some possible answers for 1 mark each. Can you add anything else? It is a very effective paragraph because … • sums up (introduced by colon) the two elements the narrator remembers of his first meeting with the Graces • opposition – girl's voice from high up/man 'here below' • reader (like the narrator) left intrigued by the noises from inside the house ('running footsteps'; the disembodied girl's voice) • the list of adjectives describing the wink culminating in 'faintly satanic' hints at the narrator's feelings of discomfort when confronted by the man ('satanic' also seems to suit the physical description earlier in the passage – the 'pointed black beard' and the reference to him being 'below') • the reader gets a clear sense that these characters will play a pivotal role in the remainder of the narrative	3
		30

Literary Study: Poetry

Answers on In a Snug Room

1.	Comment on the poet's word choice in the title of this poem. You should have been able to comment that 'snug' suggests 'sheltered'; 'cosy'; 'comfortable' (you might even have heard of the old expression 'as snug as a bug in a rug'!). 'The snug' is also the name for a separate room in an old-fashioned bar, which it makes it doubly apt in this context – 'snug' refers to both the setting of the poem and how the subject of the poem feels in the first stanza.	1

2.	'He sips from his glass' (line 1). How does the poet's language in the first stanza give you a clear impression of the sort of man 'He' seems to be?	5
	You should have been able to spot some of the following:	
	• the man is anonymous ('He') but is clearly a man of some importance; someone with a public profile ('flattering reference … morning papers')	
	• 'sips' suggests a measure of sophistication or refinement	
	• 'complacently' suggests he is self-satisfied or perhaps smug	
	• colon introduces the list of things he is pleased with	
	• 'cronies' implies close friends (although 'cronyism' now has negative connotations and a sense of corruption)	
	• 'profitable' suggests he's a successful businessman (a fat cat?)	
	• 'donation' suggests his philanthropic side – his generosity. Or is he just salving a guilty conscience?	
	• alliteration ('deal...dotted...donation') – the repeated hard plosive 'd' sounds helps to suggest the certainty of the hard headed businessman	
3.	How is the mood of self-satisfaction continued in the second stanza (lines 7–9)?	2
	'And he smiles ...' suggests further complacency – the day just seems to be getting better and better for this man. Notice how the poet deliberately leaves us guessing as to the identity of his 'true love'. Who's coming? His wife? His mistress? Someone (or something) else? – 'true love' seems a rather old-fashioned expression.	
4.	What does the poet gain from placing line 10 in a line on its own?	2
	You should have spotted that this:	
	• allows the poet to sum up succinctly the seemingly 'perfect' day being enjoyed by the man	
	• allows a dramatic pause before the climax of the poem	
5.	Comment on the effectiveness of the final three lines as a conclusion to the poem.	3
	You should have been able to comment on some of the following:	
	• placing the closing lines in a separate stanza provides a dramatic conclusion to the poem	
	• reference to 'Nemesis' gives this concise narrative a sense of 'universality' – we are invited to read it as a modern morality tale; especially when we take into account the anonymity of the central character	
	• witty juxtaposition of ancient and modern (Greek goddess and 'two bullets ...')	
	• concluding rhyme ('gun'/'one') helps to underline the final message of the poem: a warning to the self-satisfied. You might argue that this seems a peculiarly 'Scottish' response to those who are successful!	
	• the word 'gun' echoes the word 'snug' in the title (Seamus Heaney does exactly the same in his poem *Digging*)	
6.	How effectively do you think the poem's form matches its content?	2
	You could comment on:	
	• the concise form of the poem adds impact to its message	
	• free verse with no regular rhythm or rhyme for most of the poem suits the 'mini-narrative' MacCaig is telling us	
	• movement in the poem from the comfortable (literal and metaphorical) position of the anonymous man to the idea that his life is about to fall apart	

Literary Study: Drama

Answers on Long Day's Journey into Night

Answers

1.	How do the stage directions and dialogue in lines 1–15 suggest a contrast between Mary and Jamie's views of Edmund's illness? You would score 1 mark for identifying the contrast between them: Mary seems to want to believe that it is not serious while Jamie is not afraid to say what he believes is the truth: that his brother *is* seriously ill. And a further 2 marks for appropriate references plus comment. You should refer to both characters in your answer. **Mary** • *She adds nervously.* • 'A summer cold ...' as if she's downplaying its significance • *turns on him resentfully* • exclamations ('It is just a cold! Anyone can tell that! You always imagine things!') **Jamie** • (*genuinely concerned*) suggests he sees the reality of the situation • '... not just a cold' • 'The Kid is damned sick' You would also get a mark if you referred to Tyrone's attempt to placate his wife (*warning glance;* '... might have a touch of something else'). Don't forget to comment on the evidence you have selected.	3
2.	How does the dramatist suggest Mary's changing feelings in the speech beginning 'Doctor Hardy!' (line 18)? You should have spotted that she begins the speech very angrily; suggested by: • exclamation – 'Doctor Hardy!' • blunt statement – 'I wouldn't believe a thing he said ...' • exaggerated image – '... if he swore on a stack of Bibles' • short sentences suggest her conviction – 'I know what doctors are. They're all alike.' Her feelings then change to uncertainty suggested by: • repeated questions – 'What is it? What are you looking at?' • unfinished question – 'Is my hair – ?' 1 mark for identifying the change in her feelings and 1 mark for each reference plus comment you make in support of this.	3
3.	How does the dramatist explore the contrast between the past and the present in lines 27–45? You should have said something about the difference between Mary as she is now and how she was in the past. 1 mark for each of the following: • 'eyes are so bad now' • 'I did truly have beautiful hair once' • the contrasting images in the stage directions (*... not a ghost of the dead, but still a living part of her*)	3

4.	Identify the 'mood' that is established by Mary's speech beginning 'It was a rare shade ...' (line 41) and show how this mood is established.	2
	nostalgic/regretful or similar for 1 mark	
	established by:	
	• change from her pride in her hair/beauty 'rare shade/so long ...' to note of regret 'Then it began to turn to white' after Edmund's birth for 1 mark	
	• you might also have commented on the stage direction *The girlishness fades from her face.*	
5.	Explain the reason for the stage direction '(*quickly*)' in line 45.	1
	Tyrone is obviously anxious about Mary and wants to keep her spirits up (1 mark)	
	OR	
	Tyrone wants to stop her worrying about Edmund (1 mark).	
6.	What does Mary's long speech beginning 'Will you listen to your father ...' (line 46) suggest about:	
	(*a*) her relationships within the family?	2
	(*b*) her relationship with her housework and staff?	2
	(*a*) Family	
	• she seems relaxed with Tyrone and Jamie	
	• she knows when Tyrone is just trying to be nice to her ('a great actor')	
	• shares joke about Jamie's snoring ('only the foghorn')	
	• her continuing concern for Edmund ('might catch more cold')	
	(*b*) Housework and staff	
	• she seems busy 'can't stay with you any longer ... must see the cook'	
	• critical of staff ('Bridget is so lazy') yet unable to discipline them ('can't get a word in edgeways and scold her')	
	2 marks for a single fully developed point.	
	1 mark for each more basic point that you make.	
7.	Comment on the style of language used in Tyrone's comment to Jamie 'You're a fine lunkhead!' (line 60).	1
	1 mark for informal/colloquial/critical/derogatory (or similar).	
8.	Why do you think the dramatist has included the stage directions '(*slowly*)' and '(*reluctantly*)' in lines 73 and 74?	2
	'slowly' signals the seriousness or significance (or similar) of what Jamie says (1 mark)	
	'reluctantly' indicates Tyrone's unwillingness to state or acknowledge the severity of Edmund's illness (1 mark)	
9.	What are the contrasting emotions displayed by Jamie in lines 75–77?	2
	pity (for his brother) 1 mark	
	anger (directed at his father) 1 mark	
10.	How are the two different views of Dr Hardy conveyed to the audience in lines 78–87?	2
	You should have said that Tyrone defends the doctor ('always been our doctor') while Jamie uses highly critical language and imagery ('Everything's the matter with him! Even in this hick burg he's rated third class'; 'cheap old quack'). 1 mark for each explanation.	
	You might also have referred to the stage direction '*contemptuously*', which suggests Jamie's low opinion of his father's penny-pinching and, by implication, the doctor himself.	

Answers

11.	How does the language of lines 99–103 help to convey Tyrone's 'rising anger'?	3
	Any three of the following for 1 mark each: • abrupt, short sentence ('No, you can't') signals his strength of feeling • exaggeration ('I've lost all hope') • question ('You dare tell me ...?') shows he feels Jamie has overstepped the mark/ threatened his authority • repetition ('You've never ... You've never...') to drive his point home to Jamie • suggests Jamie wastes his money ('thrown your salary away') • claims moral high ground over his son ('whores and whiskey')	
12.	How does the sentence structure of lines 121–123 help to reinforce Tyrone's 'weary complaint'?	2
	You should have made mention of: • repetition ('sneer') to suggest what he feels is Jamie's critical attitude • climactic structure of the final sentence of this speech for 1 mark each.	
13.	What do Jamie's final words (line 124) suggest his about his attitude towards himself?	2
	They suggest his low opinion of himself (a good answer might refer to it as 'self-loathing') for 1 mark and a recognition that what his father says perhaps has a grain of truth in it (or similar) for the second mark.	
		30